Yale Publications in American Studies, 9

David Horne, Editor

Published under the direction of the
American Studies Program

ISHMAEL'S WHITE WORLD

A Phenomenological Reading of Moby Dick

BY PAUL BRODTKORB, JR.

NEW HAVEN AND LONDON: YALE UNIVERSITY PRESS

Copyright © 1965 by Yale University.
Second printing, December 1967.
Designed by Arthur G. Beckenstein,
set in Garamond type,
and printed in the United States of America by
The Carl Purington Rollins Printing-Office of
the Yale University Press, New Haven, Connecticut.
Distributed in Canada by McGill University Press.

Library of Congress catalog card number: 65–11176

Published with assistance from the foundation established in memory of
Amasa Stone Mather
of the Class of 1907, Yale College.

FOR LORNA

ACKNOWLEDGMENTS

MY INDEBTEDNESS HEREIN is to many people: first, to the scholars, critics, and philosophers cited in the text and footnotes, and also to several not cited. Chief among these is Charles Feidelson, Jr., my teacher, whose ideas are so pervasive that I have not footnoted appropriations from his *Symbolism and American Literature* lest the apparatus become a book in itself. Alvin Feinman first suggested the usefulness of phenomenology to me. With John Grant I have often argued *Moby Dick*. Charles McLaughlin's definition of rhetorical irony is the basis of my own formulation. Daniel Aaron, Lawrence Chisolm, R. W. B. Lewis, and Norman Holmes Pearson have each made helpful criticisms of the manuscript. Harold Bloom persistently urged me to finish it.

In my quotations of Melville I have used the Riverside Edition (Cambridge, Houghton Mifflin, 1956), edited by Alfred Kazin. The roman numerals are chapter numbers.

This book is the revised major portion of a doctoral dissertation submitted to the Yale Graduate School in 1963.

New Haven, Connecticut　　　　　　　　　　　　　　　　P. B., Jr.
August 1964

CONTENTS

INTRODUCTION

THE RHETORICAL BASIS of a first-person narrative that includes its narrator as a character is usually a variety of *apologia pro vita sua*. Because such a narrator manages more or less to justify himself in the process of evaluating his choices, acts, and involvements, he makes a specific claim on the reader's consideration. Sometimes the claim approaches an appeal for forgiveness; sometimes it is merely for as much understanding as is implicit in that desire to reveal himself which the narrator's completed book makes actual. Such "understanding" need not involve categorial reasoning; it may be no more than a "standing under" that the narrator wishes, as his very existence asks us intuitively to see him, for a while to *be* him.

Even the most perverse speakers of Poe or Dostoevski can make this claim on us, and the tendency of the relation between such a narrator and his reader is toward a kind of literary seduction. The fictive I shows us a world of conventionalized reality—of things and people and motion and time—but shows it to us in a certain way; and we may forget that in showing us this seeming uni-verse by means of language, in terms of conventions, the fictive I is already interpreting, ordering, making subjective: the seeming perception is apperception. And if we do forget this, we may be seduced too easily. Because we see as the I sees, we may passively accept the further evaluations of his vision if these pretend to be in any way normal; and the narrator has then justified himself to us, because we must agree with him.

Many writers seem to play on such ambiguous relations between the reader and the teller, and thereby demonstrate the great latitude that exists within the "normal" view of the world, the world of literary realism. For critics who are aware of this, the result can be a kind of critical paranoia: is this narrator telling the truth, is he a good man? Is Nick Carraway of *The Great Gatsby* wholly honest, as he claims, or are the nature and extent of his participation in the corrupt world he reveals to us and tries to judge more problematic than they seem? Are we to take the opinions of Hemingway's Jake Barnes at face value? Is the governess of *The Turn of the Screw* neurotic? Obviously, the answers to such fundamental questions help to determine what the critic will find in the book.

Though these questions legitimately can be asked of any personified narrator, they *must* be asked of narrators whose authority or purposes seem in any way dubious. If only because critics have seen Melville's Ishmael in so many different lights—a spectrum of illumination with, say, Lawrance Thompson at one end and Howard P. Vincent at the other—Ishmael must be counted as one of the more dubiously slippery crew.

In Ishmael's case, the matter is further complicated by his habitual use of a kind of irony that conceals its direction of reference. The traditional definition of rhetorical irony—saying the opposite of what one means—is not helpful in understanding why Ishmaelean irony is often evasive, because it keeps the area of definition within the ironical speaker. If we shift the area of definition to include the means by which a reader normally perceives that irony is intended, we can see more clearly what is at stake: rhetorical irony presents without comment a contrariety between a phenomenon in the real or fictive worlds (or in both) and what is said about it. Such irony has two broad purposes: to undercut the phenomenon, or, by silently noting the falsity of what the speaker says, to undercut the speaker's judgment. But Ishmaelean irony often blurs the necessary contrariety, because what is said is said about phenomena that are in themselves ambiguous. Radically divergent opinions of them may be held by intelligent men, with the result that virtually anything Ishmael says about such phenomena will strike certain readers as plausible and others as not. There is no sudden glare of unexpected ironical possibility unless, like Lawrance Thompson in *Melville's Quarrel with God,* one forces oneself to see it. And even then, the contrariety is by no means certified, only the possibility of it is.

Therefore one is often uncertain as to whether an Ishmaelean judgment means what it says, or (as Professor Thompson usually argues) implies its opposite, or implies both meanings somehow to be true, or implies simply the condition of ironical possibility. The consequence is that by so frequently seeming to offer us no firm standpoint, Ishmael forces the reader back upon his own resources and prevents any direct relationship: the reader cannot appropriate the Ishmaelean ironist's positive attitude in order to be a follower of or dissenter from it because the ironist offers him none to appropriate. The reader is then forced to be and to project what is in himself; and one result (though it has other causes as well) is the mountain of conflicting testimony that makes up the Melville bibliography, itself suggestive of some of the more solipsistic implications of Ishmael's Narcissus figure ("the key to it all") of *Moby Dick's* first chapter.

In short, if one usually expects to understand verbal irony immediately, here understanding must be postponed until one understands almost the totality of the phenomena at which Ishmaelean verbal ironies can point: that is, Ishmael and his fictive world. Irony, of course, is only one element in *Moby Dick* eluding precise definition.

The first step in interpreting such a book would seem to be to fix the dimensions of its phenomena. This I shall try to do in what follows by means of a descriptive analysis of the Ishmaelean consciousness; a consciousness which we, as readers, cannot escape. It constitutes for us all we can know of Ishmael and his world. My reading of *Moby Dick* will differ from other readings chiefly in its focus on the Ishmaelean consciousness through the medium of a methodological discipline specifically adapted to comprehend subjectivity, a discipline some sixty years old, and some thirty years—in France, at least—readily available—namely, phenomenology.

This formidable word, if unfamiliar to the reader, need not daunt him. Phenomenology applied to criticism assumes that arrangements of letters on a page express states of mind and thereby make manifest states of being. Thus Professor Hillis Miller (a former student of

the Belgian phenomenological critic Georges Poulet) is willing to
define literature as "a form of consciousness," and holds that "the
task of the critic is to identify himself with [the individual literary]
subjectivity expressed in words, to relive that life from the inside,
and to constitute it anew in his criticism."[1] While many critics would
wish to revise and complicate this statement of the critic's task, few,
ancient or modern, would find it irrelevant.

Despite an alien sound, "phenomenology" applied to literature
involves few really esoteric literary manipulations. Of *Moby Dick*
its use assumes no more than that what defines this book's narrator
as narrator is after all what he narrates and how he narrates it. Since
Ishmael uses the very way that he presents (that is, sees, hears, feels,
reports, judges) what he narrates in order to justify to us his total
existence, the relation that *is* his reconstitution of his world and self
is formally present in his rhetorical purpose. I shall merely try to
isolate that relation for critical inspection: I shall try to "understand" Ishmael.

An important presupposition of such an enterprise, as has already
been suggested, is not only that Ishmael is the vessel that contains the
book, but also that in a major sense he *is* the book. Given *Moby
Dick's* critical history, perhaps this presupposition needs some back-
ing up.

Melville has often been accused of violations of formal unity, as
when he is inconsistent (the Pequod's tiller sometimes has spokes,
Queequeg's island changes its name, the geographical location of
Ahab's "dismasting" shifts), or has Ishmael report things he could
not know, or lets Ishmael disappear as a character, or gives him
flights of ideas that can seem to some more Melvillean that Ishmaelean, or seems ironical at his narrator's expense. It is quite clear
that many of the book's more notorious flaws are inadvertent. I do
not deny that because the final version of *Moby Dick* was written
and revised under pressure the mistakes occurred, and that because
Melville read proof haphazardly the mistakes remained.

Nevertheless, it seems to me that literary unity is in the mental
set of the reader as much as in the literary work: as such, it is an

a priori principle of good will. Northrop Frye quotes Blake to the effect that every poem is necessarily a perfect unity, which Frye glosses as "not a statement of fact about all existing poems, but a statement of the hypothesis which every reader adopts in first trying to comprehend even the most chaotic poem ever written."[2] For the moment, this sufficiently defines the general basis of procedure in what follows.

Mistakes and inconsistencies, then, do appear in *Moby Dick,* and they are inadvertent. However, as Melville put it in *Pierre,* "when unfathomably stirred, the subtler elements of man do not always reveal themselves in the concocting act." A Freudian might extend this and argue that a writer can make "Freudian slips"; and that because he can, a writer may write better than he knows even when he blunders. Yet one need not accept the Freudian argument in order to feel that a commentator ought to consider whether or not any given blunder happens to be a fortunate one, for sheer chance makes it likely that it sometimes will be. Accidents are part of all art, often seeming to fit comfortably within its willed patterns; and for the critic not seriously to consider this possibility is at the least a premature failure of sympathy.

There is, first of all, no necessity to blame Melville for the book's inconsistencies, because most of them are storyteller's mistakes, and Ishmael is pervasively characterized as a storyteller; the mistakes, therefore, with only minimal good will on our part, might be understood as *his,* and their meaning explored in that context. Consider the extent to which this is true:

> If, then, to meanest mariners, and renegades and castaways, I shall hereafter ascribe high qualities, though dark; weave round them tragic graces; if even the most mournful, perchance the most abased, among them all, shall at times lift himself to the exalted mounts; if I shall touch that workman's arm with some ethereal light; if I shall spread a rainbow over his disastrous set of sun; then against all mortal critics bear me out in it, thou

just Spirit of Equality, which hast spread one royal mantle of
humanity over all my kind!   [XXVI]

"I shall . . . ascribe . . . weave, . . . I shall touch, . . . I shall spread"
—the active voice here says that at least some of the high qualities
are added by Ishmael for the sake of his story. Later, Ishmael admits
much the same thing:

> in this episode touching Emperors and Kings, I must not
> conceal that I have only to do with a poor old whale-hunter
> like him; and, therefore, all outward majestical trappings and
> housings are denied me. Oh, Ahab! what shall be grand in thee,
> it must needs be plucked at from the skies, and dived for in
> the deep, and featured in the unbodied air!   [XXXIII]

Other elements of the story, too, are plucked from thin air. After a
cheerfully hyperbolic sequence, Ishmael implies that he will tell
lies if necessary to make his points:

> In behalf of the dignity of whaling, I would fain advance naught
> but substantiated facts. But after embattling his facts, an advo-
> cate who should wholly suppress a not unreasonable surmise,
> which might tell eloquently upon his cause—such an advocate,
> would he not be blameworthy?   [XXV]

And like many who habitually exaggerate, Ishmael rather too often
protests his concern with accuracy: "the leading matter of it requires
to be still further and more familiarly enlarged upon, in order to be
more adequately understood, and moreover to take away any incredulity which a profound ignorance of the entire subject may in-
duce in some minds, as to the natural verity of the main points of
this affair" (XLV). But despite such protests, and often *because* of
the careful pomposity of their diction, Ishmael is sometimes not
wholly convincing. Don Sebastian in the Golden Inn in Lima, having
heard the Town-Ho's story, cannot suppress his doubts:

> Then I entreat you, tell me if to the best of your own convic-
> tion, this your story is in substance really true? It is so passing

wonderful! Did you get it from an unquestionable source? Bear
with me if I seem to press.   [LIV]

The reader's credulity also is repeatedly strained, if not in the main
points of the affair then in details: did Ahab really say to Stubb,
"Below to thy nightly grave; where such as ye sleep between shrouds,
to use ye to the filling one at last.—Down, dog, and kennel"
(XXIX)? Or is Ishmael by the majestical trappings and housings of
Shakespearean diction trying to make clear something about what
kind of status he thinks Ahab platonically has? As a character, of
course, Ishmael is a sailor, and "all sailors of all sorts are more or
less capricious and unreliable—they live in the varying outer weather,
and they inhale its fickleness" (XLVI). But formally, as narrator,
Ishmael is the storyteller, the playwright ("Enter Ahab; to him,
Stubb"), the raconteur ("Some years ago—never mind how long
precisely"); formally, he, not Melville, is the one who is inconsistent
when he does not accurately remember something he has written,
and later writes something at odds with it. Whatever the historical
truth of the matter may be, formally it is Ishmael we must judge
before we judge Melville.

If *Moby Dick,* then, can be held to reflect the mind of Ishmael,
we should not be surprised that curiously Ishmaelean traits and attitudes appear in other characters. Compare Stubb's rationalization to
Flask in his account of his dream of having been kicked by Ahab
(XXXI) with Ishmael's logic just before he turns his Presbyterian
upbringing to the idolatrous service of Queequeg's god Yojo (X).
Compare Ishmael's apostrophe to sorrow ("The sun hides not the
ocean, which is the dark side of this earth, and which is two thirds
of this earth . . . . The truest of all men was the Man of Sorrows,"
XCVI) with that of Ahab ("the gods themselves are not forever
glad. The ineffaceable, sad birthmark in the brow of man, is but the
stamp of sorrow in the signers," CVI). At such times, Ishmael imagines another character to be like himself if only because at all times
he *is* whatever character he reports, even when he reports what
logically he could not know; for he is the writer, entering into the

souls of others by virtue of his—somewhat imperfect, to be sure—Keatsean negative capability. And, similarly, when he disappears from the action, he quite simply *is* the action; why should he not be? Why should he remain a separate observer for the dubious sake of low-mimetic* unity when the existential fact he is formally demonstrating is that he was *not* separate: that he also had given himself up "to the abandonment of the time and the place"; that he, "Ishmael, was one of that crew"; that his "shouts had gone up with the rest"; that his "oath had been welded with theirs" (XLI); that in fact he and the crew "were one man, not thirty" (CXXXIV)?

As for the objections that certain flights of ideas seem Melvillean rather than Ishmaelean because they seem out of keeping with the shifty, faintly comic ex-schoolmaster and present sailor, or that certain local ironies are Melville's rather than Ishmael's, I hope in the first chapter to sketch the principle that will begin to reconcile the narrator's shiftiness with his solemnity and self-criticism. Here it need only be said, first, that any irony which seems to be Melville's directed at Ishmael (and therefore a qualification of the narrator's authority) can, without especial ingenuity, be shown to be directed by the narrator at himself as character (as narrator he has been twice-born, and he sometimes mocks his once-born self); and, second, that if we assert that at any point Melville rather than Ishmael is speaking, we are positing a second "fictional" narrator. For the I of any writing, even autobiography, is necessarily fictional, in the sense that it is a limited, selective abstraction from the total self of reality. We are positing a second fictional narrator called "Melville" whom we do not need unless, in good faith, we have tried and failed to account for the apparently Melvillean voice in terms of "Ishmael."

---

*The term, from Frye's *Anatomy of Criticism*, designates the kind of fiction that embraces "realism" and most comedy. In such fiction the hero is "superior neither to other men nor to his environment" (p. 34), while its events and formal conventions tend to reflect normality without violating the common-sense expectations of ordinary men. Frye's classification of *Moby Dick*—one which leaves much to be said—as a "romance-anatomy" (ibid., p. 313) suggests that the book may with formal legitimacy elude some of the low-mimetic conventions, of which the continuously present first-person narrator would be one.

Like the assigning of all the book's inconsistencies to Melville, this would be a premature failure of sympathy.[3]

If we are to understand the total existence called "Ishmael," we must re-experience the limits of his world, that world at which his dubious ironies point. We must again become aware that because his language evokes phenomena which can, after all, be apprehended in many ways (a "whale" may be seen with equal validity as Flask's "magnified mouse" or Job's Leviathan), *how* Ishmael perceives a phenomenon at any given moment is a kind of prereflective "choice."

Thus it is that Chapter 1 is concerned with establishing a governing principle of Ishmael's prereflective vision. Chapters 2 through 5 direct the reader's attention to the prereflective vision itself. They describe the subjective Ishmaelean universe in terms of those affective colorations that begin to constitute that universe's meaning for Ishmael; thus we describe him, or rather his prereflective, "pure" ego. In this description we grasp the prereflective I of the narrator* that by the quality of its concerns "intends"† *this particular* fictive universe into being.

Though the first five chapters are the most consistently phenomenological, whenever phenomena seem to require evaluation as well as description there will be nonphenomenological digressions. They will, however, proceed from a phenomenological basis already established. As a way of ordering the description, Chapters 2 through

*The prereflective ego of the narrator is the "I" to which any other "I" is present: that is, the fictive "I" prior to conscious reflection upon itself or its world. It is the spontaneous ego, the "I" that does the thinking, the "I" that can think about *itself* only by objectifying itself to various degrees (by, for example, assigning to itself traits of character); it is the unmediated "I" which cannot normally be grasped directly, only peripherally.

†Consciousness is intentional (according to the old scholastic formula revived and modified by Franz Brentano, developed by Edmund Husserl, and still current in one form or another in phenomenological theory) because consciousness is always consciousness *of* something: to be aware of anything at all is to "intend" it in a certain, often characterizable, way. Mind and matter are thus inseparable; subject alters, colors, and shapes what is present to it, so that "subject" and "object" spring together. To see things as closely as possible to the way in which someone else sees them is to understand that person in a radically direct way.

5 make use of the following major categories, which overlap and parallel rather than strictly exclude each other: Ishmael's existence as an intentional consciousness may be divided into his apprehension of (1) his world, excluding other people; (2) his body, and his consciousness of the bodies of others; (3) other people, including himself as character; (4) time. These categories are used because collectively, with appropriate subdivisions, they can with some show of adequacy comprehend a life-world.[4]

In Chapter 6 the focus on the Ishmaelean ego shifts. Instead of being grasped peripherally, Ishmael is now the center of our direct attention. He therefore becomes for us an "object" as his subjectivity is assigned qualities: he becomes a rounded, "opaque" character instead of a transparent narrator. The implicit events of his history are suggested. His manifest and hidden attitudes revealed in the first five chapters are analyzed and related to each other and connected with his major affects in an effort to reintegrate subject with object, narrator with character. Finally, Chapter 6 formally defines the complex emotion or sequence of emotions in which Ishmael (his book, his world, his total history) is founded.

The last chapter discusses some implications of all this in relation to Melville's literary technique. It makes plain that the chapters preceding it have added up to a structural description of Melville's symbolism in *Moby Dick,* and that they have tried to demonstrate one sort of coherence or unity[5] within this most protean of American novels.

It is clear that to treat *Moby Dick* in the fashion proposed is to inflict a twentieth-century methodology on a nineteenth-century book. If the reader is disturbed by such a procedure, I can only plead that, first, *Moby Dick* is often the source of analytic as well as descriptive material; and, second, the methodology used has itself grown out of nineteenth-century romantic thought, to the extent that its assumptions are quite compatible with Melville's as these disclose themselves in *Moby Dick.* At any rate, a subsidiary purpose of Chapter 1 is to show that my approach is not wholly anachronistic.

1. "German Metaphysics" and "Ontological Heroics"

> "what plays mischief with the truth is that men will insist upon the universal application of a temporary feeling or opinion"
> —Melville to Hawthorne, letter of June 1(?), 1851

> "Thus on all questions of significance the prior question becomes: Seen by whom, in what mood, and in what light?"
> —Rosenberry, *Melville and the Comic Spirit*

MIND ACTIVELY PARTICIPATES in the constitution of "fact." What Ishmael experiences, then reconstitutes in the form of language, is not separable from his varying states of mind. Upon such post-Kantian epistemological assumptions rests the justification of a specifically phenomenological reading of *Moby Dick*. Upon their ubiquitous presence in nineteenth-century romantic thought must rest any claim that such a reading is not finally anachronistic. No one would doubt that such assumptions were in fact available to Melville; the question is to what extent he made use of them.

I realize that in asserting the compatibility of a generally Kantian epistemology with Melville's own, I go somewhat against the conclusions of the formidable K. H. Sundermann in *Herman Melvilles Gedankengut* (Berlin, 1937), who can find little Kantian influence to speak of in Melville (see p. 109). Although several American critics hold that because of scattered references (notably in *Mardi, Redburn, Pierre,* and *Moby Dick*) Melville was acquainted with Kant's thought, no copy of Kant is cited in Merton Sealts' check list of Melville's reading, and thus there is no real indication of the degree of Melville's acquaintance. One suspects, with Sundermann, that it was probably not of the depth of a first-hand acquaintance.[1]

Yet some familiarity there must have been. William Braswell notes that the elderly Melville marked an approving reference to Kant in his copy of Schopenhauer's *World as Will and Idea*,[2] and the young Melville could hardly have avoided the many vaguely Kantian ideas dispersed during the mid-nineteenth century by the transcendentalists whom he knew so well. Perhaps at the time of *Moby Dick*, though, Melville came closest to Kantian thought in the several long conversations he had late into the night with George J. Adler, a German-American scholar, while en route to Europe aboard the same boat. Melville wrote that he was a man "full of the German metaphysics, & [who] discourses of Kant, Swedenborg &c."[3] The first series of metaphysical bull sessions took place late in 1849, and if these had any influence on Melville, we might reasonably expect to find evidence of it—even if in no other book—in *Moby Dick*, the work Melville began immediately after his return from Europe. The evidence I seek is by no means a demonstration of full-blown understanding of Kant; it is merely an indication that Melville in this one book presupposes along with "the German metaphysics" that subject stands in some partially constitutive relation to object.

The indications are at hand in the fact of Ishmael's mutability. Often his state of mind changes when his situation does, and the new state sees the same phenomena differently, as Ishmael's commentary on the story of Lazarus suggests:

> "In judging of that tempestuous wind called Euroclydon," says an old writer—of whose works I possess the only copy extant— "it maketh a marvellous difference, whether thou lookest out at it from a glass window where the frost is all on the outside, or whether thou observest it from that sashless window, where the frost is on both sides, and of which the wight Death is the only glazier." True enough, thought I, as this passage occurred to my mind . . . Poor Lazarus there, chattering his teeth against the curbstone for a pillow . . . might plug up both ears with rags, and put a corn-cob into his mouth, and yet that would not keep out the tempestuous Euroclydon. Euroclydon! says old

Dives, in his red silken wrapper . . . pooh, pooh! What a fine frosty night; how Orion glitters; what northern lights! Let them talk of their oriental summer climes of everlasting conservatories; give me the privilege of making my own summer with my own coals. [II]

Here Ishmael is suggesting that how we experience ourselves in the world is constituted in our crude condition. Thus the ordinary meaning of a port to a sailor is "safety, comfort, hearthstone, supper, warm blankets, friends, all that's kind to our mortalities"; but in a gale, to the men of a "storm-tossed ship, that miserably drives along the leeward land," "the port, the land, is that ship's direst jeopardy," because "one touch of land, though it but graze the keel, would make her shudder through and through" (XXIII); such men must view the comfortable port in horror that sees quite different aspects of it because to them in that hour in their situation it can only mean destruction.

And situation does account for Ishmael's inconsistencies, though not in quite the way he suggests in the above passages. There is something else, something *within* "situation," that influences even how "situation" itself is apprehended. Lazarus in the same situation but in another humor might be warmed by the cold of Euroclydon, apprehending it as a sign of his special worth in the eyes of God, or as a sign of imminent, hoped-for oblivion; while Dives, still physically warm, might feel the wind called Euroclydon freezing his crops or swamping his ships, and shiver in financial discomfort physically felt. Similarly, a particular sailor on a storm-tossed ship— the blacksmith of the Pequod, say, whose drinking killed his family and who as a consequence is full of "death-longing" yet still has "some interior compunctions against suicide" (CXII)—might continue to experience the port as a haven, an eternal one.

What it is that lies within "situation," determines its personal meaning, and explains differing apprehensions of similar experiences by the same consciousness may be called, for want of a better term, mood. After discussing the "peaking of the whale's flukes" prior to its dive to the sea bottom, Ishmael writes: "But in gazing at such scenes, it is all in all what mood you are in; if in the Dantean, the devils will occur to you; if in that of Isaiah, the archangels" (LXXXVI). Mood—the general affective tone, whether it has a clear name or not, the *Gestalt* of emotions—may constitute the way we experience our world. With only "a few pieces of silver," in Ishmael's pocket, his New Bedford has "hard" and "flinty" pavements: it is a world of no refuge from the "very dark and dismal night, bitingly cold and cheerless" until the subjectively ominous Spouter Inn, Peter Coffin proprietor, appears. While on an objectively quite similar night on the outward-bound Pequod, "spite of this frigid winter night in the boisterous Atlantic, spite of my wet feet and wetter jacket, it then seemed to me, many a pleasant haven in store"—here, Ishmael is warmed by anticipation: his mind is already in the south seas, where there are "meads and glades so eternally vernal, that the grass shot up by the spring, untrodden, unwilted, remains at midsummer" (XXII). Here the future is clear and inviting, and it affectively colors Ishmael's present; while in New Bedford his lack of money makes his future seem unclear, dubious, and even, for the moment, blocked. The cold weather can give him no pleasure, for there is no inner warmth to convert it. If I seem to belabor the obvious, it is because the principle asserted is both central to my later argument and the cause of much of *Moby Dick's* complexity.

If mood and world are related, it is by no means a clear question of which is prior, or of which, if either, determines the experienced character of the other. Sometimes world seems to cause mood. Even gloomy Ahab can respond to pleasant weather:

> the warm, warbling persuasiveness of the pleasant, holiday weather we came to, seemed gradually to charm him from his mood. For, as when the red-cheeked, dancing girls, April and May, trip home to the wintry, misanthropic woods; even the barest, ruggedest, most thunder-cloven old oak will at least send forth some few green sprouts, to welcome such glad-hearted

visitants; so Ahab did, in the end, a little respond to the playful
allurings of the girlish air.   [XXVIII]

Similarly, the men of the Pequod respond to a storm at sea (XL) by
fighting among themselves. Yet the final conclusion seems to be
that neither mood nor world "causes" the other, for they are connected in an ambiguous relation in which the causal values shift.
There are

> times of dreamy quietude, when beholding the tranquil beauty
> and brilliancy of the ocean's skin, one forgets the tiger heart
> that pants beneath it; and would not willingly remember, that
> this velvet paw but conceals a remorseless fang.
>
> These are the times, when in his whale boat the rover softly
> feels a certain filial, confident, land-like feeling towards the
> sea . . .
>
> The long-drawn virgin vales; the mild blue hill-sides [of the
> waves] . . . all this mixes with your most mystic mood; so that
> fact and fancy, half-way meeting, interpenetrate, and form one
> seamless whole.
>
> Nor did such soothing scenes, however temporary, fail of at
> least as temporary an effect on Ahab. But if these secret golden
> keys did seem to open in him his own secret golden treasuries,
> yet did his breath upon them prove but tarnishing.   [CXIV]

It is an interpenetrating blend, forming "one seamless whole," of
mood and world which finally characterizes world; but whenever
world is in itself ambiguous or not qualitatively insistent, then—as
with Ahab, here, whose breath of spirit tarnishes the world he experiences—mood will have the last word. Thus Moby Dick can seem
malicious to the maddened Ahab but only awkward to the even-
tempered Dr. Bunger of the Samuel Enderby. The words of the
prophet Elijah, his "diabolical incoherences," can "uninvitedly" recur to Ishmael "with a subtle energy . . . not . . . before conceived
of," and at such times "poorly could [Ishmael] withstand them."

He immediately adds, "much as in other moods I was almost ready to smile at the solemn whimsicalities of that outlandish prophet of the wharves" (XXVIII). What is at stake in this last instance is the seriousness of prophecy, and in the case of Elijah, the question is never resolved apart from the narrator's mood.

The power of moods is so great that it can determine how we experience ultimates. Here is Ishmael confronting the idea of death:

> In what census of living creatures, the dead of mankind are included; why it is that a universal proverb says of them, that they tell no tales, though containing more secrets than the Goodwin Sands; how it is that to his name who yesterday departed for the other world, we prefix so significant and infidel a word, and yet do not thus entitle him, if he but embarks for the remotest Indies of this living earth; why the Life Insurance Companies pay death-forfeitures upon immortals; in what eternal, unstirring paralysis, and deadly, hopeless trance, yet lies antique Adam who died sixty round centuries ago; how it is that we still refuse to be comforted for those who we nevertheless maintain are dwelling in unspeakable bliss; why all the living so strive to hush all the dead; wherefore but the rumor of a knocking in a tomb will terrify a whole city. All these things are not without their meanings.   [VII]

One implication of this passage is that after the first death there is no other; that death is an *absence,* a void. Indeed, the mere possibility of what man often claims he hopes for—life after death ("the rumor of a knocking in a tomb")—is enough to terrorize the living; because their truest, most spontaneous reaction is to feel horror in death, not "unspeakable bliss." Ishmael's procedure throughout this passage is to argue from what the ordinary, unreasoned emotions and habits of man in the face of death are, to what these imply about death's nature (a nature at hypocritical odds with reasoned religious belief). Ishmael's procedure, in other words, is circular: it begins and ends with the emotions, upon which the habits are founded—

these are his only evidences for the "meanings" he sinisterly implies. He cannot get beyond these feelings that parallel his own gloom to the pure phenomenon of death, so that death exists for him here only as the human meanings of moods.

Then, as if to drive home the point, Ishmael adds: "But Faith, like a jackal, feeds among the tombs, and from even these dead doubts she gathers her most vital hope." Sitting in the whaleman's chapel, facing the memorial tablets, Ishmael himself illustrates this as a mood of optimism inexplicably takes possession of him:

> But somehow I grew merry again. Delightful inducements to embark, fine chance for promotion, it seems—aye, a stove boat will make me an immortal by brevet. Yes, there is death in this business of whaling—a speechlessly quick chaotic bundling of a man into Eternity. But what then? . . . Methinks my body is but the lees of my better being. In fact take my body who will, take it I say, it is not me. And therefore three cheers for Nantucket; and come a stove boat and stove body when they will, for stave my soul, Jove himself cannot. [VII]

Two moods in quick succession result here in polarized views of death: death is final and horrible; death is immortality and is not to be feared. One may of course suspect that the view of death conditioned by the first mood is more generally congenial to Ishmael, because the bravado of the second mood, expressing itself climactically in the chapter's final words—"Jove himself cannot" (Jove is an archaic, a dead, god, and therefore has no present power at all)— rings more than faintly hollow, and suggests that the narrator-Ishmael in re-presenting for us this particular mood shift of the character-Ishmael is being ironic at the expense of his former self. Yet it is clear that for his former self the polar views of death were equally *true* at the successive moments in which they were held. And because the character Ishmael changes his mind with his mood, it becomes possible to think that the narrator Ishmael may change his moods sometimes, and thereby change self and world.

"Emotion," says Jean-Paul Sartre, "is a certain way of apprehending the world";[4] and consciousness does not just project affective
significance on the world around it, it *lives* the "new" world which
it has in part created, for it believes in that world which is for the
moment the only world it has.[5] As William James notes, the phenomenon of the "eternal recurrence of the common order, which so
fills a Whitman with mystic satisfaction, is to a Schopenhauer . . .
the feeling of an 'awful inner emptiness' from out of which he views
it all."[6] The contemporary Dutch psychologist Van den Berg agrees:
"What a man sees, hears, tastes and smells in the very first place
concerns himself."[7] As Melville put it in *Pierre:* "Say what some
poets will, Nature is not so much her own ever-sweet interpreter, as
the mere supplier of that cunning alphabet, whereby selecting and
combining as he pleases, each man reads his own peculiar lesson
according to his own peculiar mind and mood." Or, as Ishmael puts
it:

> in mountainous countries where the traveller is continually
> girdled by amphitheatrical heights; here and there from some
> lucky point of view you will catch passing glimpses of the
> profiles of whales defined along the undulating ridges.

And immediately he adds:

> But you must be a thorough whaleman, to see these sights . . .
>   [LVII]

To see whales, one must be a whaleman. Truly to see the white
whale, one must, for a while at least, be Ishmael in his several
moods, or, as he calls them as early as the book's first paragraph,
his "hypos"; because in the beginning as in the end it is the stage
of subjectivity on which Melville plays out the "ontological heroics"[8]
of *Moby Dick.*

2. World: Materiality—Earth, Air, Fire, and Water

MY OBJECT in this chapter is to note the few basic attitudes that Ishmael holds with relative consistency toward earth, air, fire, and water, attitudes which could obviously be extended and refined (and in fact have been in Melville criticism) but which here will constitute a kind of minimal phenomenology of the elements, in the sense that any more extensive interpretive elaboration of them always has to take these Ishmaelean attitudes into account.

Land life tends toward the stable and the certain. Earth is the domain of the *familiar:* therefore, in one mood land can seem "safety, comfort, hearthstone, supper, warm blankets, friends, all that's kind to our mortalities" (XXIII); it is where "the wife, the heart, the bed, the table, the saddle, the fire-side, the country" (XCIV) are. In a contrary mood, however, the familiar seems aggressively boring: one is forced to turn one's gaze away from the contemplation of earth and become "fixed in ocean reveries" as a necessary respite from "week days pent up in lath and plaster—tied to counters, nailed to benches, clinched to desks" (I). The *forms* of earth are confining. Even "green fields" (I) will not do for refreshment, because they too are part of earth. Islands may be exempted from the several condemnations of this mood, but islands are a very special instance of "earth": though *formed,* and sharing some of earth's comforts, they are set in oceans, and men on islands are not very far from the sea or likely to be out of touch with the sea's values— islands are both less homelike and less boring than continental masses. But because they mediate between the values of land and sea, islands are too bland to satisfy the extreme mood of one who would spurn the "slavish shore" (XXIII), "the turnpike earth!—that common highway all over dented with the marks of slavish heels and boots" (XIII). For such a man, nothing will do but going to sea.

One goes to sea intending to get away from that mood in which land encompasses the familiar, the boring, the superficial, the static, the deadly, the too definitively formed, because the sea provides the elemental contrast with the land: its waters take what little form they have from the land, but only at edges and bottom, so that their total form is hidden; they are fluid, changeable, not static substance; they have multileveled depths, not just surfaces; they are interesting, not boring. "Interesting," for the sea is the domain of the *strange,* not the familiar, and therefore going to sea opens "the great flood-gates of the wonder world" (I). One goes to sea to see that world.

Because one does, as soon as the decision to go to sea is made one's jaded interest revives. Literally, one's horizons widen, as they always do when visiting a foreign country: one sees *more,* and differently (though perhaps not more profoundly). The sense of life is renewed. The earth-world itself seems more interesting as earth becomes the borders of the sea: the strange becomes more noticeable as it mixes with the familiar: strolling down New Bedford streets, one observes

> actual cannibals stand chatting at street corners; savages outright; many of whom yet carry on their bones unholy flesh. It makes a stranger stare.   [VI]

Here, even the familiar (this is after all still the realm of earth) begins its sea transformation into the strange:

> But besides the Feegeeans, Tongatabooarrs, Erromanggoans, Pannangians, and Brighggians, and, besides the wild specimens of the whaling-craft which unheeded reel about the streets, you will see other sights still more curious, certainly more comical. There weekly arrive in this town scores of green Vermonters and New Hampshire men. . . . Look there! that chap strutting round the corner. He wears a beaver hat and swallow-tailed

coat, girdled with a sailor-belt and sheath knife. Here comes another with a sou'-wester and a bombazine cloak.   [VI]

As the domain of the strange, that which attracts our interest and intellect ("meditation and water are wedded for ever"), the sea will seem boring only to a wholly practical nonthinker like the ex-sailor Peleg, through whose eyes Ishmael momentarily sees when he answers Peleg's question as to what the water-world looks like:

Going forward and glancing over the weather bow, I perceived that the ship . . . was now obliquely pointing towards the open ocean. The prospect was unlimited, but exceedingly monotonous and forbidding; not the slightest variety that I could see.   [XVI]

Ishmael begins to reassert his original interest in the sea, however, when he reports to Peleg what he saw:

"Not much . . . nothing but water; considerable horizon though, and there's a squall coming up, I think."

Here Ishmael gently mocks his former eager interest, and foreshadows something of the *emptiness* and brooding violence of the water-world that will reappear later in a somewhat different sense than the one initially suggested by Peleg's question. But it is also important to notice that the view here is of the sea-*horizon*—its surface, not its depths; for, later, the depths of the sea will be revealed as the home of terrible prodigies whose terrors, in distinction from the merely "comprehensible" terrors of land, are "interlinked . . . [with the] wonders of God" (XXXIV) so often that "in a whaler wonders soon wane" (L).

Once actually at sea, one finds that the strange is always present, even when the waters seem mildest and most landlike, and the ship "seems struggling forward, not through high rolling waves, but through the tall grass of a rolling prairie" and "you almost swear

that play-wearied children lie sleeping in these solitudes, in some
glad May-time, when the flowers of the woods are plucked" (CXIV):

> There is, one knows not what sweet mystery about this sea,
> whose gently awful stirrings seem to speak of some hidden soul
> beneath; like those fabled undulations of the Ephesian sod
> over the buried Evangelist St. John. And meet it is, that over
> these sea-pastures, wide-rolling prairies and Potters' Fields of
> all four continents, the waves should rise and fall, and ebb and
> flow unceasingly; for here, millions of mixed shades and
> shadows, drowned dreams, somnambulisms, reveries; all that
> we call lives and souls, lie dreaming, dreaming, still; tossing
> like slumberers in their beds; the ever-rolling waves but made
> so by their restlessness.   [CXI]

Yet such earthlike friendliness, sweetly touched with mildly
estranging, restless mystery, is finally a cheat:

> Consider the subtleness of the sea; how its most dreaded
> creatures glide under water, unapparent for the most part, and
> treacherously hidden beneath the loveliest shades of azure. Con-
> sider also the devilish brilliance and beauty of many of its most
> remorseless tribes, as the dainty embellished shape of many
> species of sharks. Consider, once again, the universal cannibal-
> ism of the sea; all whose creatures prey upon each other, carry-
> ing on eternal war since the world began.   [LVIII]

Such a world sheltering such creatures is predominantly masculine
rather than feminine, hard rather than soft. It is feminine chiefly in
its deceits, which might more accurately be called feline, for it is a
"tiger heart that pants beneath" those "hearth-stone cats," the soft
waves, that "purr" against the gunwales of small boats (CXIV);
whatever else is feminine in it resembles either a "stepmother" in
being "cruel" and "forbidding" (CXXXII) or the queen of the "dark
Hindoo half of nature" whom Ahab worships as the goddess of his
"darker faith" and who speaks to him "too truly . . . in the wide-
slaughtering Typhoon" (CXVI). It is only appropriate that such a

world is peopled by men, and that women exist in it only as an absent principle, to be longed for sentimentally (CXXXII) or lasciviously ("There's naught so sweet on earth—heaven may not match it—as those soft swift glances of warm, wild bosoms in the dance, when the over-arboring arms hide such ripe, bursting grapes," XL). For men there is no female intercession in this world.[1]

It is also appropriate that the natural creatures of the water-world are unlike earth creatures, familiar and predictable:

> Indeed, in other respects, you can hardly regard any creatures of the deep with the same feelings that you do those of the shore. For though some old naturalists have maintained that all creatures of the land are of their kind in the sea; and though taking a broad general view of the thing, this may very well be; yet coming to specialities, where, for example, does the ocean furnish any fish that in disposition answers to the sagacious kindness of the dog? The accursed shark alone can in any generic respect be said to bear comparative analogy to him.
>
> [LVIII]

Water level being below land level, the creatures of water behave accordingly, having little in common with any except the most ferocious of land creatures. Sometimes there is no relation at all: the sea at any moment can reveal some utterly strange horror like the giant squid: "No perceptible face or front did it have; no conceivable token of either sensation or instinct; but undulated there on the billows, an unearthly, formless, chance-like apparition of life" (LIX). It is precisely the "un-earthly" formlessness of such water creatures, reflecting the basic formlessness of water itself, that is the source of their horror for the mind; just as, apprehended (in the more inclusive, distanced version of the mood) as "the strange," it is the source of their interest, for interest and horror are modes of positive and negative motions of the engaged mind. Thus "meditation and water are wedded for ever" (I) because thought itself (considered apart from "water") is characteristically an attempt to master its own contents by forming them into patterns; therefore in relation to water it is exactly the *formlessness* of water becoming the contents of the mind that invites meditation and its attendant patterning.

First, water-formlessness seduces the mind to blend in with its own fluidity, and "every strange, half-seen, gliding, beautiful thing" in it "seems . . . the embodiment of those elusive thoughts that only people the soul by continually flitting through it" (XXXV). In this phase of seduction it provides relaxation from the rigors of patterned and patterning thought—the mind just drifts; but perhaps because the normal mind eventually will move out of total passivity to some kind of active exploration and direction of its thoughts, the formlessness of water thoughts and water creatures eventually becomes a kind of affront to thought itself, and finally a challenge to mind to exercise its proper powers. But whenever, as in the case of the giant squid, the massive formlessness of water creatures insists too much on the actuality of their lack of form, the defeated mind may retreat in the face of this something that totally resists rationalization; and it may retreat in "horror" because intractable formlessness denies the validity of the mind's very basis for being.

On land as on sea "ignorance is the parent of fear" (III), but at sea some ignorance is invincible, therefore some horror inevitable. On land the *predictability* of forms implies both comfort and boredom; if one leaves earth for water, one must accept the interlinked terrors and wonders of water creatures and water thoughts: their aggressive strangeness as well as their passive strangeness.

Because the strange attracts that pattern-imposing thought which hopes to bring the strange at least a little nearer to the domain of the familiar, one might well be tempted to classify "the constituents of a chaos" (XXII) if one were committed to thought. Yet the creatures of the sea like squids and whales *are* finally a chaos as far as man can tell and they resist all classification:

> In various sorts of whales, they [the parts] form such irregular combinations; or, in the case of any one of them detached, such an irregular isolation; as utterly to defy all general methodiza-

tion . . . On this rock every one of the whale-naturalists has
split.   [XXXII]

Like the giant squid, whales cannot be comprehended in terms of
static images because their features do not accept forms:

> For all these reasons, then, any way you may look at it, you
> must needs conclude that the great Leviathan is that one creature
> in the world which must remain unpainted to the last. True,
> one portrait may hit the mark nearer than another, but none
> can hit it with any very considerable degree of exactness. So
> there is no earthly way of finding out precisely what the whale
> really looks like. And the only mode in which you can derive
> even a tolerable idea of his living contour, is by going a whaling
> yourself . . .   [LV]

By going whaling you may get closer to the whale and derive a
tolerable idea of him, but that "idea" is at best a hurriedly blurred
view of the whale as a mysteriously animated object; understanding
the whale subjectively by grasping the whale's view of things is impossible because even its modes of perception differ too radically
from man's:

> the eyes [of most other animals, including man] are so planted
> as imperceptibly to blend their visual power, so as to produce
> one picture and not two to the brain; the peculiar position of
> the whale's eyes, effectually divided as they are by many cubic
> feet of solid head, . . . must wholly separate the impressions
> which each independent organ imparts. The whale, therefore,
> must see one distinct picture on this side, and another distinct
> picture on that side; while all between must be profound dark-
> ness and nothingness to him.   [LXXIV]

The whale's view of things is so different from man's that man cannot imaginatively appropriate it:

> any one's experience will teach him, that though he can take
> in an undiscriminating sweep of things at one glance, it is quite

impossible for him, attentively, and completely, to examine any
two things . . . at one and the same instant of time . . . But if
you now come to separate these two objects, and surround each
by a circle of profound darkness; then, in order to see one of
them, in such a manner as to bring your mind to bear on it, the
other will be utterly excluded from your contemporary consciousness.   [LXXIV]

It is in part because of its strange "diametrically opposite powers of
vision," resulting in a "helpless perplexity of volition," that the
whale behaves at times in spontaneous ways impossible to predict
(LXXIV). In short, subjective, empathic understanding of the whale
is not effective. Nor is genuinely objective understanding: to analyze
the whale or even his parts is futile:

The more I consider this mighty tail, the more do I deplore my
inability to express it. At times there are gestures in it, which,
though they would well grace the hand of a man, remain
wholly inexplicable. . . . Nor are there wanting other motions
of the whale in his general body, full of strangeness, and un-
accountable to his most experienced assailant. Dissect him how
I may, then, I go but skin deep; I know him not, and never will.
But if I know not even the tail of this whale, how understand
his head? much more, how comprehend his face, when face
he has none? Thou shalt see my back parts, my tail, he seems
to say, but my face shall not be seen. But I cannot completely
make out his back parts; and hint what he will about his face,
I say again he has no face.   [LXXXVI]

Monumental formlessness and unpredictable spontaneity can defeat the mind's comprehension. But there is a further reason for the
failure of analysis to find or create forms in the aggressively formless.
It is suggested in two of the preceding quotations* that the total
whale exists only *in process.* What follows develops that suggestion:

*The one immediately preceding, and the second one on p. 25, above.

How vain and foolish, then, thought I, for timid untravelled man to try to comprehend aright this wondrous whale, by merely poring over his dead attenuated skeleton, stretched in the peaceful wood. No. Only in the heart of the quickest perils; only when within the eddyings of his angry flukes; only on the profound unbounded sea, can the fully invested whale be truly and livingly found out. [CIII]

Here is the final resistance of nature to thought: thought-forms, systems of analysis, deal in categories, and categories are static, while nature—that to which the categories are applied—is always in process. Ultimately, it is because process can wear no fixed forms that the whale can have no true face.

It is for much the same reason that Queequeg's island is "not down on any map; true places never are" (XII): maps are the most abstractly analytic and static kind of image for nature (one might compare Redburn's useless map of Liverpool in this respect: the city has changed since his old map was drawn). Only images of nature which through their *suggestiveness* begin to partake of the idea of process can begin to be adequate; thus, for example, the domain of water can perhaps be imaged most accurately as a kind of violent mystery, as in the Spouter Inn's painting that provides an image invoking the active mental participation of the onlooker in order to show itself as made up of any forms at all.

No more than mind, then, does nature stand still, though mind would like it to. But since it will not stay itself for mind's convenience, nature will always more or less elude the necessary rigidity of analytic forms of thought:

All the trees, with all their laden branches; all the shrubs, and ferns, and grasses; the message-carrying air; all these unceasingly were active. Through the lacings of the leaves, the great sun seemed a flying shuttle weaving the unwearied verdure. Oh, busy weaver! unseen weaver!—pause!—one word!—whither flows the fabric? what palace may it deck? wherefore all these ceaseless toilings? Speak weaver!—stay thy hand!—but one

single word with thee! Nay—the shuttle flies—the figures float
from forth the loom; the freshet-rushing carpet for ever slides
away.   [CII]

If endless process is the condition of even vegetable land-nature,
which so often at least seems to accept static forms, how much more
true must it be of sea-nature, which shares not only water's formlessness but its *motion:* gliding, elusive, an analogue of process.* Formless and (in Whitman's phrase) in eternal transfer and promotion,
water creatures are like their element: though they invite meditation,
they finally defeat it.

Hence, of course, Ishmael's satires against philosophers, for these
are men who build systems that impose the static on the processional.
Ishmael as would-be systematizer says, "I promise nothing complete;
because any human being supposed to be complete, must for that
very reason be faulty" (XXXII).[2] Humorously diffident about *his*
system of classifying whales, he is aware that philosophical complete-
ness is a kind of fraud and that the best architects of the truest con-
structions "ever leave the copestone to posterity." If nature is incomplete, so must systems be.

Even the simplicities and familiarities of nature can elude analysis.
Water, the element of seductive elusiveness, combines with another
common but mysterious element, air, to produce a mixture which also
defeats categorizing thought:

> You have seen him [i.e. the whale] spout; then declare what
> the spout is; can you not tell water from air? My dear sir, in
> this world it is not so easy to settle these plain things.   [LXXXV]

Because the formlessness, spontaneity, and processional motion of
the water-world is at least *material,* some *thing* is present to the
mind to be the object of its attention and interest. This minimal
objectification is perhaps necessary to seduce thought, for it is difficult to think about what is not at least vaguely visualizable.

*Another quotation suggesting the universality of "process" is given below,
p. 36.

Like water, air, too, is formless; and in the guise of wind it has motion. But it is nonmaterial; the mind cannot visualize it. The behavior of air is equally as mysterious as that of water, but it constitutes a mystery the mind is rarely tempted to solve because there is literally no *thing* for the mind to apprehend. Nevertheless, air has certain phenomenal features that suggest the characteristics of the realm of air: chiefly, it is invisible, existing as a kind of all-encompassing, spontaneously animated Being. As Ahab says:

> 'tis a noble and heroic thing, the wind! who ever conquered it? In every fight it has the last and bitterest blow. Run tilting at it and you but run through it . . . Would now the wind but had a body; but all the things that most exasperate and outrage mortal man, all these things are bodiless as objects, not as agents. There's a most special, a most cunning, oh, a most malicious difference!   [CXXXV]

What Ahab means by wind having body as an agent is suggested by his earlier outburst to Starbuck: "By heaven, man, we are turned round and round in this world, like yonder windlass, and Fate is the handspike" (CXXXII). Wind has body in the sense that it can bodily affect material objects: it provides the prime force for motion over the water-world. When it is sufficiently violent, it can wholly determine a ship's speed and direction of motion, regardless of any efforts to modify these that the crew might make:

> In tempestuous times like these, after everything above and aloft has been secured, nothing more can be done but passively to await the issue of the gale. Then Captain and crew become practical fatalists.   [LI]

It is for such reasons that Ahab experiences wind as fate and the agent of the gods. So, for the same reasons, does Ishmael:

> The hand of Fate had snatched all their souls; and by the stirring perils of the previous day; the rack of the past night's suspense; the fixed, unfearing, blind, reckless way in which their wild

craft went plunging towards its flying mark; by all these things, their hearts were bowled along. The wind that made great bellies of their sails, and rushed the vessel on by arms invisible as irresistible; this seemed the symbol of that unseen agency which so enslaved them to the race.   [CXXXIV]

To experience wind in this way accords with its phenomenal character. The gods, too, are invisible, and make their home in the sky, and, despite their nonmateriality, are all-powerful. Potential emissaries from the gods—lightning, storms, strange vindictive birds[3]— ride on the air. The gods, like air, cannot be quiescently manipulated by objectifying thought, for their wholly conjectural forms are unseen; the mind cannot grasp them, nor does it find much profit to try. Air, like the gods, transcends mere earth and water existence. Like the gods it is capricious in its behavior, sometimes "feminine" and "mild" (CXXXII) when it seems to favor our enterprises, sometimes dangerously malevolent. But when Tashtego is hinted to be "a son of the Prince of the Powers of the Air" (XXVII), it is clear that the powers in question are not there for our good.

Like air, fire seems nonmaterial and transcendent, resembling nothing else in the world. Unlike air, it is visible. These qualities seem contradictory: visible but nonmaterial and transcendent, fire is therefore a phenomenal mystery which preeminently unites contrary associations.

For example,* at the tip of a flame, where the color almost ceases to be and becomes sheer vibration, fire is *spirit;* yet this spirit exists at the expense of some ordinary, material fuel. Fire's tendency is to leap up, heavenward; yet it comes from below. It cooks meat and thereby vanquishes putrefaction, it separates substances, it consumes material impurities; yet it leaves behind ashes.

Confronted with this mystery, gazing at flames, the mind becomes a state of wonder and reverie. It is no accident that primitive men worshiped fire, and that primal men like Fedallah[4] still do. But

---

*My examples are taken from *La Psychanalyse du feu,* by Gaston Bachelard, Paris, 1937.

what such worship of fire makes of fire reflects fire's duality: fire burns in hell and shines in heaven; it tortures as well as illuminates.

In the Ishmaelean world, light is the most important characteristic of fire. Because light illuminates, it is "explanatory" (CVI). The hunter of whales is fortunate in that he burns "the purest of oil, in its unmanufactured, and, therefore unvitiated state"; he "goes and hunts for his oil, so as to be sure of its freshness and genuineness" (XCVII); his job is to seek "the food of light" and "he lives in light" (XCVII) in contrast to the merchantman sailor and the land man. Though the whaleman lives in light, he should not trust the light of those flames which illuminate from below:

> as their uncivilized laughter forked upwards out of them, like the flames from the furnace; as to and fro, in their front, the harpooneers wildly gesticulated with their huge pronged forks and dippers; as the wind howled on, and the sea leaped, and the ship groaned and dived, and yet steadfastly shot her red hell further and further into the blackness of the sea and the night .... then the rushing Pequod, freighted with savages, and laden with fire, and burning a corpse, and plunging into that blackness of darkness, seemed the material counterpart of her monomaniac commander's soul.
>
> So it seemed to me, as I stood at her helm, and for long hours silently guided the way of this fire-ship on the sea. Wrapped, for that interval, in darkness myself, I but better saw the redness, the madness, the ghastliness of others. [XCVI]

While light may be explanatory, the light from these flames is not to be trusted because it adds its color to the scene, color which would not be there without its presence:

> Look not too long in the face of fire, O man! . . . believe not the artificial fire, when its redness makes all things look ghastly. [XCVI]

Because light is that quality in fire which idealizes it, as well as what, coming *from* fire, illuminates, any fire which is pure, uncolored

light—consuming no fuel and leaving no ashes—is literally unearthly; which is why it is sent from above by the gods. But because
the illumination of such fire is only momentary, incomplete, and
usually against a vast background of darkness, such light can be no
everyday guide either. Problematic as its light may be, though, fire
like this is clearly sacramental and requires a priest-interpreter. It
comes in a personal way only to such men, like Ahab, who worship it
(Ahab says of a dying whale, "He too worships fire" [CXVI]) and
it seems to speak to them in some way, perhaps because the inner
intensity of such "godlike" (XVI) men reflects and corresponds to
its own intensity. Ahab's important speech to this kind of fire (CXIX)
is therefore its definitive explication, at least insofar as man *can*
explicate it. Which is not very far, because the illumination of such
perfectly idealized fire amounts to "clear Truth," which is "a thing
for salamander giants only to encounter" (LXXVI); such fire is
mythic, emblematic of those ultimate revelations direct from the
gods which are too much for human mortality to bear: "What befell
the weakling youth lifting the dread goddess's veil at Sais?" (LXXVI).

It is the sun—perhaps because as fire it is intense, flooding, and
formed—that provides the only light to be trusted even hesitantly.
Eventually it illuminates all sides of man's world:

> To-morrow, in the natural sun, the skies will be bright; those
> who glared like devils in the forking flames, the morn will
> show in far other, at least gentler, relief; the glorious, golden,
> glad sun, the only true lamp—all others but liars!
>
> Nevertheless the sun hides not Virginia's Dismal Swamp,
> nor Rome's accursed Campagna, nor wide Sahara, nor all the
> millions of miles of deserts and of griefs beneath the moon. The
> sun hides not the ocean, which is the dark side of this earth, and
> which is two thirds of this earth.   [XCVI]

The sun is preeminently natural light, and is here apparently con-
trasted with mechanical, artificial, and conjuring fires; with fires such
as Ahab's in which he has his harpoons forged—artificial fires with
which to fight natural fire. But the rhetoric of the first of the two

paragraphs just quoted is so extravagant ("the glorious, golden, glad sun, the only true lamp!") that it resembles previous hyperboles like "Jove himself cannot,"* and like them suggests a kind of self-mockery. It does so even more if we remember an earlier analysis of light which suggested that white light, though it shows all sides impartially, is far from accurate: like the false, reddening light of flames, neutral sunlight colors the world, and is all the more treacherous in that it seems not to; for on this earth every object colored other than white is falsely colored:

> all other earthly hues—every stately or lovely emblazoning— the sweet tinges of sunset skies and woods; yea, and the gilded velvets of butterflies, and the butterfly cheeks of young girls; all these are but subtle deceits, not actually inherent in substances, but only laid on from without; so that all deified Nature absolutely paints like the harlot, whose allurements cover nothing but the charnel-house within; and when we proceed further, and consider that the mystical cosmetic which produces every one of her hues, the great principle of light, for ever remains white or colorless in itself, and if operating without medium upon matter, would touch all objects, even tulips and roses, with its own blank tinge—pondering all this, the palsied universe lies before us like a leper.   [XLII]

Finally, even the sun is not to be trusted as a source of light.

Nor is it to be trusted in itself. Not only does it deceitfully color objects upon which its light falls, but it burns those who would honor it. When Ahab says, "Cursed be all things that cast man's eyes aloft to that heaven, whose live vividness but scorches him. . . . Level by nature to this earth's horizon are the glances of man's eyes" (CXVIII), he speaks what he knows from experience. Always the "circus-running sun" that races within its "fiery ring, and needs no sustenance" but what is in itself (LXXXVII) keeps its own counsel. Sunlight seems good, yet it is the treacherous Fedallah who is the

---

*See above, p. 17.

book's formal sun worshiper, and he is, perhaps (according to certain "uncanonical Rabbins"), a child of the devil, a product of those ancient times when "devils . . . indulged in mundane amours" (L). If, like Ishmael, we "must look at this matter in every light" (CV), we must also remember that light itself does not guarantee truthful vision if the sun remains, like all fire, a dangerous mystery.

Indeed, even the unassertive moon may be classed as that. Like the sun it is formed; unlike the sun it gives off only pale, reflected light. But what it mildly lights remains mysterious, tantalizing, and, sometimes, sinister:

> It was while gliding through these latter waters that one serene and moonlight night, when all the waves rolled by like scrolls of silver . . . a silvery jet was seen far in advance of the white bubbles at the bow. Lit up by the moon, it looked celestial; seemed some plumed and glittering god uprising from the sea. Fedallah first descried this jet.   [LI]

Finally, if we can trust Ahab's intuition, the mystery that all light signifies may be of something beyond itself: "There is some unsuffusing thing beyond thee, thou clear spirit [of fire], to whom all thy eternity is but time, all thy creativeness mechanical" (CXIX). In vain does the dying whale "seek intercedings with yon all-quenching sun, that only calls forth life, but gives it not again" (CXVI). Even Ishmael has moments in which he feels that beyond fire live "vindictive princes and potentates," just as in air may dwell "the unseen, ambiguous synod" (CVI).

World: Spatiality—Motion through Matter

Earth-bound men engage in water-reveries as they face the sea. Mentally, they move from fixity into a mobile realm of interest. When one of these men goes to sea in actuality, he is giving physical expression to a prior mental motion.

As the sea is approached by way of New Bedford and Nantucket, strange portents appear. Earth seems to confront the would-be voyager with dark meanings; the domain of the stable and the familiar takes on the character of the impenetrable, which nevertheless mysteriously points beyond itself in time. Matter seems filled with omens whose meanings are either rejected or felt to be uncertain as they are experienced, though the passage of time may seem to grant them validity and clarity. Matter thus seems indistinct, unstable: physiognomic but blank, distant but portentously near. As the sea is approached, night and storm become the favored conditions of earth.

To go to sea is to articulate an exploratory mental motion into a night journey.[5] For some, this would be a choice; for others, a necessity. Those who find it the latter experience travel as a "substitute for pistol and ball" (I); as, literally, an alternative to death. For such men, motion *is* the opposite of stasis, and something none but the mentally or actually dead can avoid. Such men experience the world as a place through which one *must* move.

Thus Ishmael is a man who has made travel his life; home, despite passages that may seem to suggest the contrary,[6] is what he has left for good. To inhabit the world under these circumstances is to inhabit an inn rather than a home:

> It is but well to be on friendly terms with all the inmates of the place one lodges in.   [I]

> But I am one of those that never takes on about princely fortunes, and am quite content if the world is ready to board and lodge me, while I am putting up at this grim sign of the Thunder Cloud.   [XVI]

> But when a man's religion becomes really frantic; when it is a positive torment to him; and, in fine, makes this earth of ours an uncomfortable inn to lodge in, then I think it high time to take that individual aside and argue the point with him. [XVII]

To be in the world is for Ishmael to inhabit an inn because being itself is most typically experienced as travel: as motion only momentarily interrupted by static respite. Like process, motion char-

acterizes the living and denotes their essential difference from the
dead.

But motion in this world is primarily horizontal motion, over
land and water, and because these two elements make up one "terraqueous globe" (XIV) such motion is necessarily circular; in the
world one must "circumnavigate," and circumnavigation, however
necessary, has its dreary aspects:

> whereto does all that circumnavigation conduct? Only through
> numberless perils to the very point whence we started, where
> those that we left behind secure, were all the time before us.
> [LII]

It is the roundness of the world that gives this character to most
motion:

> Were this world an endless plain, and by sailing eastward we
> could forever reach new distances, and discover sights more
> sweet and strange than any Cyclades or Islands of King Solo-
> mon, then were there promise in the voyage. But in pursuit of
> those far mysteries we dream of, or in tormented chase of that
> demon phantom that, some time or other, swims before all
> human hearts; while chasing such over this round globe, they
> either lead us on in barren mazes or midway leave us whelmed.
> [LII]

Because such motion, though seemingly necessary, often is felt as
futile, one may long for rest:

> Would to God these blessed calms would last. But the mingled,
> mingling threads of life are woven by warp and woof: calms
> crossed by storms, a storm for every calm. There is no steady
> unretracing progress in this life; we do not advance through
> fixed gradations, and at the last one pause:—through infancy's
> unconscious spell, boyhood's thoughtless faith, adolescence'
> doubt (the common doom), then scepticism, then disbelief, rest-
> ing at last in manhood's pondering repose of If. But once gone

through, we trace the round again; and are infants, boys, and
men, and Ifs eternally. Where lies the final harbor, whence we
unmoor no more?   [CXIV]

Because such circumnavigation can suggest a kind of endless nullity,
"the round world itself" can in certain moments seem "but an empty
cipher" (XCIX).

Besides the endlessness of circumnavigation, there is also the more
intense horizontal rotation of the vortex. Perhaps at the center of
this circular motion which at least *has* a reachable center is to be
found the longed-for stasis, something like the calm at the center
of the circling, frenzied school of whales:

> And thus, though surrounded by circle upon circle of consterna-
> tions and affrights, did these inscrutable creatures at the centre
> freely and fearlessly indulge in all peaceful concernments; yea,
> serenely revelled in dalliance and delight. But even so, amid
> the tornadoed Atlantic of my being, do I myself still for ever
> centrally disport in mute calm; and while ponderous planets
> of unwaning woe revolve around me, deep down and deep in-
> land there I still bathe me in eternal mildness of joy. [LXXXVII]

This is one possibility that might be found at the center of a vortex.
But there is another:

> For so revolvingly appalling was the White Whale's aspect,
> and so planetarily swift the ever-contracting circles he made,
> that he seemed horizontally swooping upon them. And though
> the other boats, unharmed, still hovered hard by; still they
> dared not pull into the eddy to strike, lest that should be the
> signal for the instant destruction of the jeopardized castaways,
> Ahab and all . . .   [CXXXIII]

Because at the center of *that* vortex stasis is ultimate, what is at the
horizontal center of "the vortex" must remain uncertain.

Yet the vortex is one instance of a logical way out of horizontal,
circular motion, however ambiguous a way it is, for a vortex on the

sea surface is a circular movement of water with a vacuum at the
center. Its tendency is to suck down (it is a vortex that finally sucks
down the Pequod and her crew and almost pulls in Ishmael); because it behaves in this fashion it suggests one pole of the two possibilities of vertical motion which would allow escape from "the
endlessness, yea, the intolerableness of all earthly effort" (XIII) that
horizontal circularity involves.

The other possibility is upward movement. Moving upward is at
odds with horizontal movement:

> The strange, upheaving, lifting tendency of the taffrail breeze
> filling the hollows of so many sails, made the buoyant, hovering
> deck to feel like air beneath the feet; while still she rushed
> along, as if two antagonistic influences were struggling in her
> —one to mount direct to heaven, the other to drive yawingly
> to some horizontal goal.   [LI]

Moving upward is to leave the surface of the world, as in climbing
a mast or a pyramid: "that the Egyptians were a nation of masthead
standers, is an assertion based upon the general belief . . . that the
first pyramids were founded for astronomical purposes" (XXXV).
Moving upward is to aspire, finally, to some static, ultimate knowledge of and identity with Being:

> lulled into such an opium-like listlessness of vacant, unconscious
> reverie is this absent-minded youth [on the mast-head] by the
> blending cadence of waves with thoughts, that at last he loses
> his identity; takes the mystic ocean at his feet for the visible
> image of that deep, blue, bottomless soul, pervading mankind
> and nature; and every strange, half-seen, gliding, beautiful
> thing that eludes him; every dimly discovered, uprising fin of
> some undiscernable form, seems to him the embodiment of
> those elusive thoughts that only people the soul by continually
> flitting through it. In this enchanted mood, thy spirit ebbs away
> to whence it came; becomes diffused through time and space . . .
>   There is no life in thee, now, except that rocking life im-

parted by a gently rolling ship; by her, borrowed from the sea; by the sea, from the inscrutable tides of God.   [XXXV]

But this is only an exceptional moment stolen from the endless flux of time and from circular, horizontal motion. As soon as movement, time, and identity return, the stasis is broken:

But while this sleep, this dream is on ye, move your foot or hand an inch; slip your hold at all; and your identity comes back in horror. Over Descartian vortices you hover. And perhaps, at mid-day, in the fairest weather, with one half-throttled shriek you drop through the transparent air into the summer sea, no more to rise for ever.   [XXXV]

What awaits the climber, who must one way or another eventually come down, is the vortex, with *its* ambiguous possibility of escape from horizontal circularity. And the possibility of descent—since although what goes up must come down, what goes down needn't come up—represents a more real because more permanent escape than ascent. Yet in major respects the other pole of verticality is similar: like ascent, descent involves self-dissolution in favor of reaching an identity with Being, in this case by becoming part of the "hidden soul" beneath the water's surface (CXI).[7] Like ascent, the end of such becoming means also knowledge of Being: Ahab strives "to pierce the profundity" (CXXXII) because for him, as for Ishmael, to descend is "to have one's hands among the unspeakable foundations, ribs, and very pelvis of the world" (XVI). In the standard romantic pattern of *Faust, Endymion,* and *Prometheus Unbound,* to descend is to find "deeper wonders" (XVI): it is perhaps nothing less than to find ultimate truth, an inconceivable realm in which thought and being are perfectly congruent; for if "all truth is profound" (XLI), it is to the very deepest reaches that the vortex pulls, and it pulls precisely away from life's round of time, process, and circular motion.

This is why whales are used by Ishmael not only to mock philosophers but to suggest real profundity. Whales are free to move vertically as well as horizontally: in the act of peaking its flukes, the whale's "gigantic tail seems spasmodically snatching at the highest heaven" from "out of the bottomless profundities" (LXXXVI); similarly, the sperm whale can be accounted "no common, shallow being, inasmuch as it is an undisputed fact that he is never found on soundings, or near shores; all other whales sometimes are" (LXXXV). Like "Plato, Pyrrho, the Devil, Jupiter, Dante" (LXX), the whale "is both ponderous and profound" (LXXXV). If whales can be said to be *like* such thinkers in that they are fond of profundities, they are *unlike* them in that they can *live* at these depths among their ultimate truths—because neither water nor fire can be man's elemental home, the inmost character of each supports just that sort of ultimate truth inaccessible to man: whales can live in the depths and are therefore outsize philosophers; clear Truth is the property of salamander giants living in fire. Ahab assumes that whales' truths are not the varieties of falsification that are the truths of philosophers when he addresses the head of a sperm whale:

> Speak, thou vast and venerable head, . . . which, though ungarnished with a beard, yet here and there thou lookest hoary with mosses; speak, mighty head, and tell us the secret thing that is in thee. Of all divers, thou hast dived the deepest. That head upon which the upper sun now gleams, has moved among the world's foundations.   [LXX]

The head, of course, does not speak. Such deep, static truth is not knowable by living man, for the whale's truth can be humanly experienced only in the stasis of death, as by the Pequod's crew, or in the ambiguous stasis of madness,[8] as by Pip:

> carried down alive to wondrous depths, where strange shapes of the unwarped primal world glided to and fro before his passive eyes; and the miser-merman, Wisdom, revealed his hoarded heaps; and among the joyous, heartless, ever-juvenile eternities, Pip saw the multitudinous, God-omnipresent, coral insects, that out of the firmament of waters heaved the colossal orbs. He saw God's foot upon the treadle of the loom, and spoke

it; and therefore his shipmates called him mad. So man's insanity is heaven's sense; and wandering from all mortal reason, man comes at last to that celestial thought, which, to reason, is absurd and frantic ... [XCIII]

The "thought" (either that man's insanity is in itself heaven's sense —i.e. heaven's sense is chaos—or that reason cannot know *what* heaven's sense is without first wandering far from sanity) is celestially far from mortal reason if only because the truth that Pip knows, whatever its character,[9] is not communicable except by a language no sane man can fully comprehend, and which man-made language itself cannot relate. Men speak to men, but Pip is no longer a complete man: his soul is elsewhere, still in the sea, "drowned" so that only his "finite body" (XCIII) is left ("Have ye seen one Pip?" what remains of Pip asks over and over again, since Pip is no longer *here*). Pip knows the final truth because by virtue of his self-dissolution part of him has become one with Being; he has in this experience felt "the drawing near of Death" and been impressed with the "last revelation." Were he literate, he might even aspire to be "an author from the dead" and "adequately tell" (CX) his revelation; but such an author has not yet existed, and if one miraculously did, he could not speak to living men because of the great gulf between him and them; so Pip "feels . . . indifferent as his God" (XCIII), and his language is the language of God, the language of riddles and parables, the language of that deepest truth which cannot be faced without mediation, that truth which on the surface of the "seas of life" (XLI) is not understandable: "For whatever is truly wondrous and fearful in man, never yet was put into words or books" (CX), and "Wonderfullest things are ever the unmentionable" (XXIII).

Such truth as Pip must know is ultimate, because descent, unlike ascent, can finally break the chain of time, process, and circular motion. Such truth is not the truth of ordinary life, where being is becoming and rational thought systems cannot be congruent with the flux of matter. In the end, successfully to escape circular horizontality is either to die or to go mad.

3. BODY

ISHMAEL SEES THE SOUL as a kind of ghost animating the body, and therefore I shall use his word "soul" as phenomenally corresponding to the self: the inmost, spontaneously animated consciousness; or (as on page 9 above), the prereflective I (pure, transparent ego, *to* which all objectified personality is present, itself not objectifiable or reducible to anything else). This arbitrary correspondence of self and soul keeps open major metaphysical questions: the soul may or may not have eternal life, be capable of reincarnation etc., but as the personal, present self it always behaves as my usage of the word "self" suggests, whatever characteristics beyond the limits of the immediate self it may or may not (outside of the temporal world) prove to have.

What allows one to exist in and move through the world is one's body, an entity that is almost the same as, yet is clearly different from, the self; the personal animating principle, which many call the soul. Body is almost the same as self, because a man whose body is sick is himself sick: suddenly told by a doctor that he has, say, cancer, a man's world changes, his experience of time changes, reflecting the change in his body as his body reflects the change in him. Similarly, a mother by the bedside of her sick child caressing the child's arm does not stroke part of a machine inhabited by her essential, spiritual child; she touches the child itself.[1] In the sense that what happens to the body happens to the man, man *is* his body. Man is his body in health as well as sickness, in a kind of easy, prereflective way: performing any action unself-consciously, the dancer does not exist apart from the dance, nor the body apart from the self that uses it to perform.

Sometimes, though, man *has* his body, and it is *not* himself. A sick man protesting his sickness is no longer quite "a sick man"; he rebels against being his body, that awkward hulk which will not do what *he* wants it to and which therefore is not, could not be, he, but which circumstances seem to insist *is* he. His refusal to accept his body as himself resembles Sartrean bad faith (the self-deception that consciousness engages in prereflectively); for if time decides for the success of his rebellion, it will do so only to reunite self and body into an identity the sick man will accept. But it is not wholly bad faith; for as soon as one's body is made the object of one's thought, it becomes different from whatever it is one most essentially *is*. This is true in health as well as in sickness, and the relationship between body and self in either state may be summed up as follows: the body is the self whenever it is taken for granted and is not an object for consciousness; it differs from the self whenever the self is estranged from it by being conscious *of* it.

Obviously, most of the time the body is not an object for consciousness, it simply *is*. When it is thereby very closely related to the self, its general condition reflects the state of the self; a careful observer accurately noting the appearance of someone's body will be able to tell a lot about him. Because "the soul is glued inside of its fleshy tabernacle, and cannot freely move about in it, nor even move out of it, without running great risk of perishing" (XXXV), the body is intimately related to the soul; what affects one will affect the other:

> I labored to show Queequeg that all these Lents, Ramadans, and prolonged ham-squattings in cold, cheerless rooms were stark nonsense; bad for the health; useless for the soul; opposed, in short, to the obvious laws of Hygiene and common sense. I told him, too, that he being in other things such an extremely sensible and sagacious savage, it pained me, very badly pained me, to see him now so deplorably foolish about this ridiculous Ramadan of his. Besides, argued I, fasting makes the body cave in, hence the spirit caves in; and all thoughts born of a fast must necessarily be half-starved. This is the reason why most dyspeptic religionists cherish such melancholy notions about their hereafters. [XVII]

The passage is argumentative hyperbole, yet the same relation of soul to body is seriously advanced as an explanation of Ahab: "his torn body and gashed soul bled into one another; and so interfusing, made him mad" (XLI). Similarly, Ahab's vision of the world is repeated in his physical state: "The White Whale swam before him as the monomaniac incarnation of all those malicious agencies which some deep men feel eating in them, till they are left living on with half a heart and half a lung" (XLI). Finally, "you cannot hide the soul" (X). The "lean brow and hollow eye" marks an inner being "given to unseasonable meditativeness" (XXXV). The body and face conspire to show forth the self:

> When Bildad was a chief-mate, to have his drab-colored eye intently looking at you, made you feel completely nervous, till you could clutch something—a hammer or a marling-spike, and go to work like mad, at something or other, never mind what. Indolence and idleness perished before him. His own person was the exact embodiment of his utilitarian character. On his long, gaunt body, he carried no spare flesh, no superfluous beard, his chin having a soft, economical nap to it, like the worn nap of his broad-brimmed hat. [XVI]

Starbuck, too, is expressed in his body:

> He was a long, earnest man, and though born on an icy coast, seemed well adapted to endure hot latitudes, his flesh being hard as a twice-baked biscuit. Transported to the Indies, his live blood would not spoil like bottled ale. . . . Only some thirty arid summers had he seen; those summers had dried up all his physical superfluousness. But this, his thinness, so to speak, seemed no more the token of wasting anxieties and cares, than it seemed the indication of any bodily blight. It was merely the condensation of the man. . . . His pure tight skin was an excellent fit; and closely wrapped up in it, and embalmed with inner health and strength, like a revivified Egyptian, this Starbuck seemed prepared to endure for long ages to come. . . . [XXVI]

Because "real strength never impairs beauty or harmony, but often bestows it; and in everything imposingly beautiful, strength has much to do with the magic" (LXXXVI), when Bulkington is described in terms of "noble shoulders, and a chest like a coffer-dam," and "brawn" that is "seldom seen . . . in a man," the whole adding up to a uniquely "fine stature" (III), all this is clearly part of his characterization: as a man, he has bulk. Ishmael himself is "of the broad-shouldered make" (XVI), and the implication of inner and outer health is the same:

> A thin joist of a spine never yet upheld a full and noble soul. I rejoice in my spine, as in the firm audacious staff of that flag which I fling half out to the world.   [LXXX]

This is one truth about the harmonious, unconscious relation of body to soul and self; but there is the opposite truth, which depends on the moment of self-conscious perception of the body as a thing that one *has,* the moment in which the self is not the body. Ahab, whose body is always potentially falling short of what his will requires from it and who is thereby compelled to be aware of his body as *separate,* knows this part of the truth to the exclusion of the other:

> "—But even with a broken bone, old Ahab is untouched; and I account no living bone of mine one jot more me, than this dead one that's lost. Nor white whale, nor man, nor fiend, can so much as graze old Ahab in his own proper and inaccessible being. . . .
>
> "Oh, oh, oh! how this splinter gores me now! Accursed fate! that the unconquerable captain in the soul should have such a craven mate!"
>
> "Sir?"
>
> "My body, man, not thee. . . . 'Tis Ahab—his body's part; but Ahab's soul's a centipede, that moves upon a hundred legs."
>
>   [CXXXIV]

Ahab asserts his body to be different from his soul, but precisely because he feels his body to be continually so inadequate to and estranged from his inmost volition, Ahab is "crazy Ahab" (XLI). Pip,
too, exhibits the same disjunction—"The sea had jeeringly kept his
finite body up, but drowned the infinite of his soul" (XCIII)—and
Pip, too, is called mad. For body and soul continually to be felt as
estranged from each other is to be insane.

There are, however, at least two instances in the book where
Ishmael seems to maintain the normality of the separation of body
and soul. One is the passage quoted on page 17 above, wherein
Ishmael, foreshadowing Ahab's argument quoted on the preceding
page, asserts "come a stove boat and a stove body when they will, for
stave my soul, Jove himself cannot" (VII); but this passage in context
seems to represent Ishmael being gently ironic at the expense of a
former self and opinion of his, and the opinion is never given convincing dramatic validity in the book, whereas the normal congruence
of body and soul repeatedly is. Similarly, when Ishmael at the first
sight of the outlandish Queequeg reassures himself with the observation "It's only his outside; a man can be honest in any sort of skin"
(III), he immediately adds, "But then, what to make of his unearthly
complexion, that part of it, I mean, lying round about, and completely independent of the squares of tatooing." Ishmael's misgivings
are instant, and after closer observation and acquaintance, he goes
on to reverse his opinion about the nonpertinence of Queequeg's
appearance to:

> Savage though he was, and hideously marred about the face—
> at least to my taste—his countenance yet had a something in
> it which was by no means disagreeable. You cannot hide the
> soul. Through all his unearthly tatooings, I thought I saw the
> traces of a simple honest heart; and in his large, deep eyes, fiery
> black and bold, there seemed tokens of a spirit that would dare
> a thousand devils.   [x]

In short, normally body reflects self, but body requires careful and accurate observation to reveal self; and what is revealed may be ambiguous.

Thus Ahab's insistence on the absolute disjunction between body and self is more a part of Ahab's perspective than Ishmael's. Moreover, however unwilling Ahab may be to accept his body as a manifestation of his inmost identity, other people do, if only because his body itself denotes the schizophrenic split between his body and soul:

> Threading its way out from among his grey hairs, and continuing right down one side of his tawny scorched face and neck, till it disappeared in his clothing, you saw a slender, rod-like mark, lividly whitish. It resembled that perpendicular seam sometimes made in the straight, lofty trunk of a great tree, when the upper lightning tearingly darts down it, and without wrenching a single twig, peels and grooves out the bark from top to bottom . . . [XXVIII]

Despite his felt estrangement from his body, for an outside observer Ahab's body unmistakably expresses him:

> He looked like a man cut away from the stake, when the fire has overrunningly wasted all the limbs without consuming them, or taking away one particle from their compacted aged robustness. His whole high, broad form, seemed made of solid bronze, and shaped in an unalterable mould, like Cellini's cast Perseus. . . .
>
> I was struck with the singular posture he maintained. Upon each side of the Pequod's quarter-deck . . . there was an auger hole . . . His bone leg steadied in that hole; one arm elevated, and holding by a shroud; Captain Ahab stood erect, looking straight out beyond the ship's ever-pitching prow. There was an infinity of firmest fortitude, a determinate, unsurrenderable wilfulness, in the fixed and fearless, forward dedication of that glance. [XXVIII]

Ahab's intolerable existential position is suggested by his legs:

> While his one live leg made lively echoes along the deck, every
> stroke of his dead limb sounded like a coffin-tap. On life and
> death this old man walked.   [LI]

The very movements of his body[2] express him: "And, so full of his
thought was Ahab, that at every uniform turn that he made, now at
the main-mast and now at the binnacle, you could almost see that
thought turn in him as he turned, and pace in him as he paced; so
completely possessing him, indeed, that it all but seemed the inward
mould of every outer movement" (XXXVI).

    The congruence of self and body cannot be evaded. Inspection of
the visible form will reveal the invisible mold. But just how much of
this invisible mold does the outside reveal? Queequeg, we are told,
is "always equal to himself" (X); and his face and body express him.
His tattoos further reveal him (Ishmael also is tattooed, as he suggests
in chapter CII; but since his are never seriously shown us, they give
us no hint of his inner self beyond what he admits in chapter LVII:
"I myself am a savage . . ."). Yet what do they reveal about Queequeg,
these legs "marked, as if a parcel of dark green frogs were running
up the trunks of young palms" (III)? The general significance may
be roughly paraphrased, but the translation can never be more than
approximate:

> This tattooing, had been the work of a departed prophet and
> seer of his island, who, by those hieroglyphic marks, had written
> out on his body a complete theory of the heavens and the earth,
> and a mystical treatise on the art of attaining truth; so that
> Queequeg in his own proper person was a riddle to unfold; a
> wonderful work in one volume; but whose mysteries not even
> himself could read, though his own live heart beat against them;
> and these mysteries were therefore destined in the end to
> moulder away with the living parchment whereon they were
> inscribed, and so be unsolved to the last.   [CX]

The outside reveals and expresses the inside, yet what that inner significance may be in its full nature and extent remains finally inscrutable:

> Champollion deciphered the wrinkled granite hieroglyphics. But there is no Champollion to decipher the Egypt of every man's and every being's face. Physiognomy, like every other human science, is but a passing fable.   [LXXIX]

Ahab, so fully expressed by his body, is nevertheless a mystery:

> This is much; yet Ahab's larger, darker, deeper part remains unhinted. But vain to popularize profundities, and all truth is profound.   [XLI]

Indeed, "touching all Ahab's deeper part, every revelation partook more of significant darkness than of explanatory light" (CVI); this is true if only because under the present bodily surface lies a kind of primeval self, remote in time and inwardness:

> Winding down from within the very heart of this spiked Hotel de Cluny where we here stand—however grand and wonderful, now quit it;—and take your way, ye nobler, sadder souls, to those vast Roman halls of Thermes; where far beneath the fantastic towers of man's upper earth, his root of grandeur, his whole awful essence sits in bearded state; an antique buried beneath antiquities, and throned on torsoes! So with a broken throne, the great gods mock that captive king; so like a Caryatid, he patient sits, upholding on his frozen brow the piled entablatures of ages. . . . and from your grim sire only will the old State-secret come.   [XLI]

Which is why "no man can ever feel his own identity aright except his eyes be closed; as if darkness were indeed the proper element of our essences, though light be more congenial to our clayey parts" (XI).

To summarize: the self is near, yet remote; it is whole, yet it may, like Ahab's (and that of most of the other major characters at one time or another), itself be split; it is stable, yet, as Stubb once says when charged by Flask with inconsistency: "I've part changed my flesh since that time, why not my mind?" (CXXI). We are left with the contradictory observation with which we began: the body is the self, and the body is not the self. Both statements are true, forming a closed circle from which there is no escape.

4. Others: The Basic Relation

Since body only partially and ambiguously reveals self, to some extent the selves of others must remain mysterious to Ishmael, finally hidden behind the indecipherable hieroglyphs of the material forms of the body. Now, what is mysterious is in some measure estranged. We can socialize with it if we choose, but our encounter with it, whether it strikes us as radically or only slightly estranged, will involve degrees of ambivalent tensions: the *other* is holding something back, and we may respond by holding something back from the other. "Call me Ishmael," says the friendly, talkative narrator to his reader-auditor as he begins his story; then he goes on, "Some years ago—never mind how long precisely"; and in the sudden slight retreat from the friendly opening is defined for us the basic relation of self to other.

The separation between narrator and reader so quickly suggested goes on to become the fundamental relation between the narrator and the other characters, even between the narrator and himself as character. An edgy alternation of emotional advance and retreat, this dance of estrangement requires that the perceiving self be always *outside,* a spectator, a voyeur, however much the self might wish to become more completely engaged with those separated from it.

Others: Roles

At its most extreme, the separation of self from other seems immutable, not part of an ever-shifting process of relationship at all. Then, everyone seems cut off from everyone else. The crew of the Pequod are "nearly all Islanders . . . *Isolatoes* . . . not acknowledging the common continent of men, but each *Isolato* living on a separate continent of his own" (XXVI). This condition is reflected in the most typical means of character presentation: little set-piece essays like those grouped in the two chapters (but found throughout the book) called "Knights and Squires" that introduce each new character, describing and interpreting him, then going on to the next, as if each man were caught within his own small space, alone, connected with other men only artificially and by convention. Indeed, even the blank verse soliloquies, which F. O. Matthiessen held to be flaws insofar as "each one distracts attention to itself and interferes with the singleness of . . . development,"[1] contribute to the effect of isolating the characters.

Against all such apparent isolation and inertia it seems a major achievement that men can come together in any sort of purposive, self-transcending movement; but somehow they do, becoming "federated along one keel" (XXVI) under a captain's orders; and in this perspective on the human condition,

> Who ain't a slave? Tell me that. Well, then, however the old sea-captains order me about . . . I have the satisfaction of knowing that . . . everybody else is one way or another served in much the same way—either in a physical or metaphysical point of view, that is; and so the universal thump is passed around, and all hands should rub each other's shoulder-blades, and be content.   [I]

Men come together to work, which is just one more "uncomfortable infliction that the two orchard thieves entailed upon us" (I); it is by working to get money to buy food that men can stay alive. Work is payment and punishment, endlessly weary:

> Oh! my friends, but this is man-killing! Yet this is life. For hardly have we mortals by long toiling extracted from this world's vast bulk its small but valuable sperm; and then, with weary patience, cleansed ourselves from its defilements, and learned to live here in clean tabernacles of the soul; hardly is this done, when—*There she blows!*—the ghost is spouted up,

and away we sail to fight some other world, and go through
young life's old routine again. [XCVIII]

This being the character of work, it is only common sense that
men should "rub each other's shoulder-blades" and seek to ease the
pain of necessary labor with alternate rhythms of shared effort and
relaxing companionship. But work goes beyond this. Splendid isolation does get broken up into motion and relation in order for work
to get done; but then, having become federated into a productive
society, a man may be dismayed to find that he has somehow come
to be utterly dependent on other men, each man bound to each by
a kind of societal monkey-rope of specific social roles:

> I seemed distinctly to perceive that my own individuality was
> now merged in a joint stock company of two; that my free will
> had received a mortal wound; and that another's mistake or
> misfortune might plunge innocent me into unmerited disaster
> and death. . . . And yet still further pondering . . . I saw that
> this situation of mine was the precise situation of every other
> mortal that breathes; only, in most cases, he, one way or an-
> other, has this Siamese connexion with a plurality of other
> mortals. If your banker breaks, you snap; if your apothecary by
> mistake sends you poison in your pills, you die. [LXXII]

Men may be isolated, but in their isolation they are caught up
with each other's aloneness into a corporation built out of social
roles (banker, apothecary, captain, sailor); and they are caught up
with one another for more reasons than mere food-getting survival:
society exists not only for the sake of work, but also for the mutual
protection of its members against the treacherous world of nature,
full of threats and horrors. At any time a storm may blow up, a man
may fall overboard; and against this context the social world is "a
mutual, joint-stock world, in all meridians" in which "we cannibals
must help these Christians" (XIII). Here, society might almost be
defined as a humanly willed violation of the physical and metaphysical isolation of otherness, for the purpose of saving lives. As

such, it is on the one hand the book's formal, ethical response to the apparent fact of nonethical nature; and on the other, a kind of schematization and simplification of the essential relation of man to man and self to other.

But because society in its sense of human brotherhood is a willed simplification for a moral purpose, it cannot be fully congruent with the total, complex reality of human existence. Any account of the layers of human existence and human relation below that of social roles must deal with fluidity and change, and present the finally mysterious self as (in Søren Kierkegaard's formula) a relation that relates itself to itself, as well as show this processional entity in relation to other selves. And this last relation, as Ishmael's first address to the reader suggests, is a kind of estrangement wherein the self remains always outside of the other, but does manage to approach and retreat in halting, measured steps.

Others: The Dance of Estrangement

The movement of self in relation to others has in *Moby Dick* four chief manifestations, two of them attempts to transcend isolation, one a wry acceptance of it, and one a synthesis of transcendence and acceptance. First, the mysterious self that animates the other may be felt to be capable of some *explanation* that will dissolve the mystery and ease the ambiguous tensions of relation. Thus, before Queequeg appears, the innkeeper tells "the most mystifying and exasperating stories" (III) about him, and it is precisely the mystery that exasperates; but when the mystery—here a simple and mechanical one—is explained, the more profound mysteries remain, and Queequeg is "unsolved to the last" (CX). Similarly, before Ahab appears, Ishmael "felt impatience at what seemed like mystery in him" (XVI); but, again, the deeper part can only be dimly perceived and conjectured about, never explained away. Because "ignorance is the parent of fear" (III) and because Ishmael fears ignorance (the entire book records the monumental efforts he has made to educate himself at all levels), Ishmael is initially a person who demands "a satisfactory answer concerning what [seems] mysterious" in others (III), a persistent rationalizer of the mysterious in others; and a persistently defeated one.

There are, it is true, moments when perfect communication seems possible. Love, at least, can bridge the gap. The other then seems to become a "thou," rather than a "you" or a "he" or an "it."[2] Ishmael can "marry" Queequeg and sit with him in the dark so that the vexing sign-and-barrier of the body becomes less self-insistent, and then:

> see how elastic our stiff prejudices grow when love once comes to bend them. For now I liked nothing better than to have Queequeg smoking by me, even in bed, because he seemed to be full of such serene household joy then. . . . I was only alive to the condensed confidential comfortableness . . .   [XI]

But it is important to note that this is only one night; that it takes place in the dark, not the light; and that it is reported to us in such a way that we have to take Ishmael's word for it: *we* never get inside Queequeg's essential self, or even very close to him. For us he remains throughout the book just as mysterious as Ishmael in fact presents him to be. If Ishmael in an expansive mood sometimes suggests that Queequeg is really no mystery, at those times he does not quite compel our belief; or, rather, he cannot help us to bridge the gulf between ourselves and Queequeg the gentle headhunter, even if he has for an instant bridged it himself. Love may be a bridge, but what it crosses over to is as incommunicable as the ultimate truths Pip saw in the depths of the sea.

Rationalizing explanation, then, though often tried, conspicuously fails to disperse the estranging mystery of others; and love is only momentarily, incompletely, and ambiguously successful. A third way of confronting otherness is fully to accept it as itself, beginning at the level of perception. To accept it means in part to accept one's own condition as that of voyeur, outsider, traveler *through* the world. Otherness is thereby dramatized, and its end of the self-other spectrum remains an oddly animate substance: people distanced, seeming like puppets without a puppeteer in view. Initially, this mode of experiencing otherness is represented conventionally by means of characters who seem almost Dickensianly grotesque animated *objects:* the early, antic Ishmael defending his choice of going to sea; Peter Coffin planing a bench for Ishmael's bed; Mrs. Hosea Hussey offering a choice of chowders; Peleg and Bildad arguing. These are all comic characters, opaque, mildly played for laughs because, as Stubb on the foretop (and therefore, perhaps, close to some degree of illumination) says, "a laugh's the wisest, easiest answer to all that's queer" (XXXIX); a laugh emotionally distances us from what we laugh at, a laugh accepts and answers the mystery. The other is seen so often as comic in part because he *is* the other.

Even Father Mapple may be seen as a character "comic" in his estrangement and distance, as he pulls up his singular ladder to withdraw himself spiritually from the congregation before delivering in allusively expansive language the sermon none of his congregation will understand. Because this view of Father Mapple is at odds with that of most Melville criticism, I should like here to digress to a consideration of his language, the keynote of which is incongruity.

Though Father Mapple's language is perhaps the major means by which he is characterized, the full nature of the character it suggests has not been sufficiently explored. A fair example of Mapple's prose is this: "no friends accompany him [Jonah] to the wharf with their adieux." Considering Jonah's situation, the last word here is a minor Sophoclean irony; "good-bye" would, of course, be equally that, but the fashionable French word is jarring enough in context to call attention to its literal meaning. Father Mapple's language is shot through with just this sort of meaningful absurdity, and one point seems to be that he is not fully conscious of the cumulative tone of his style. He means it to be colloquial, and there is colloquial effectiveness in it, but there is also a basic inappropriateness to the subject matter of his sermon in that he dramatizes the mythically remote miracle story of Jonah in anachronistically everyday terms, which could seem the desperate rhetorical strategy of a preacher anxious to popularize his distant material for his audience of hard-headed practical sailors, were Father Mapple not clearly a man of integrity. Nevertheless, his style, by covertly underplaying the miraculous, tends to deny the absolutely exceptional nature of the Jonah story, so that it becomes party to a kind of sentimental lie, as well as itself always being on the verge of unintended comedy. In this way the effectiveness of Father Mapple's rhetoric does not seem quite under his control; and as the style runs away from the speaker, one result for those who notice it is to distance ironically his sermon.

I would therefore argue that Father Mapple's language is a clue pointing to his basically comic nature, even though he *is* taken seriously by the dead-pan narrator-character Ishmael (the character takes him seriously; the narrator noncommittally reproduces the absurd sermon style); and that consequently the sermon itself is not to be solemnly valued for its pious content over, say, Fleece's more pragmatic sermon (equally uncomprehended by *its* audience) to the sharks—in fact, in the societal dimension of the book, at least, Mapple's ethical-religious imperatives have less actual relevance for either social good or evil than Fleece's more obviously comic sermon. Fleece's sermon fails because sharks do not understand his language; Mapple's fails for similar reasons: spiritually withdrawn from his audience, as the retracted ladder suggests, Mapple, despite his strenuously colloquial dramatizations, ends his sermon in a series of non sequiturs, heroic admonitions (hyperbolic in relation to those actually there, though for a man like Ahab they would not be), and dark hints of personal sin, all of which must have baffled his audience (the notably tolerant Queequeg leaves before the end)—the effect of which is to confirm the exaggerations of his style in dramatic action.

I do not mean to assert here that total religious commitment is not taken seriously as an existential possibility—it clearly is in the case of Ahab—merely that Father Mapple's style of religious commitment as borne witness to by his sermon style has been subtly undermined by the language conveying it, and though what he says is said in church, the reader should not allow any suspension of disbelief induced by churchly receptivity to blind him to the several absurd elements present here. I realize that in all this I argue counter to not only Melville criticism in general but F. O. Matthiessen in particular, a dangerous man to disagree with. Matthiessen finds Mapple's sermon to be in the "metaphysical style"[3] and wholly successful. Yet even Matthiessen betrays a certain hesitancy when he remarks after an extended quotation from Mapple, "The schemata of that rhetoric may seem at first reading uncomfortably elaborate."[4] My contention is that Matthiessen's first reading is as valid as his second thoughts. His quotation of Emerson's remark about Father Edward Taylor, Mapple's probable model in the real world, sheds some light on the whole problem: "Emerson . . . was still aware that Taylor's discourse had no more method than he had quite accidently and 'ludicrously copied and caricatured from the old style, as he found it in some Connecticut tubs' ";[5] it seems to me that Melville, always more alive to incongruities than Emerson, has in Mapple's sermon style retained some of the ludicrous spirit of the original. And if he has, the reader is faced with a sermon whose sacramentalism is almost neutralized by its style in a tenuous balance of elements serious and absurd. In short, we need take Father Mapple's sermon no more, or less, seriously than any given speech of Peleg, Stubb, Flask, or Ishmael. Though comic characters often speak Melvillean truths ("And the man that has anything bountifully laughable about him," says Ishmael in chapter V, "be sure there is more in that man than you perhaps think for"), those truths must stand or fall by themselves in the total context.

If Mapple is comic in the sense developed here, he is so because he is experienced as radically different and distanced from Ishmael; and what he says has little relevance *to* Ishmael (though, of course, a great deal to Ahab). Ishmael cannot appropriate the sermon in Father Mapple's terms, he can only reproduce it.[6]

The fact of otherness may of course be accepted without being seen in a comic mode. The native harpooners, Fedallah, and the "tiger yellow" (XLVIII) Manillas of Ahab's boat crew are all kept far from the reader, yet seem disturbingly near by virtue of their portentousness. In their shifting, unresolved distance from us, they resemble those strange, natural animate objects of the sea that have the quality of the numinous which attracts and repels at once. The harpooners' strange, natural tattoos (Queequeg's legs, it will be recalled, are "marked as if a parcel of dark green frogs were running up the trunks of young palms") or markings ("Fedallah was calmly eyeing the right whale's head, and ever and anon glancing from the deep wrinkles there to the lines in his own hand" [LXXIII]) indicate how much a part of this sort of nature they are; like Fedallah, they are creatures such "as civilized, domestic people in the temperate zone only see in their dreams" (L). There is a sense, of course, in which the entire crew of the Pequod, indeed even the reader, is "natural"—Ishmael asks, "who is not a cannibal?" (LXV) and admits "I myself am a savage" (LVII); Ahab calls himself "cannibal old me" (CXXXII)—but such naturalness merely suggests potentiality for savage behavior. In addition to it, men show degrees of sympathetic attunement to the rhythms and forces of nature, and it is those natives most attuned who strike us as most completely and mysteriously *other*.

They seem as self-sufficient as nature itself; they don't need us or our understanding for completion. Like Queequeg, men experienced by us in this mode are content with their own companionship and always equal to themselves (X). To us, they seem *unconscious* (XIII) because they act spontaneously, prereflectively, according to the natural demands of the situation, of which they are instinctively and instantly aware (as when Queequeg rescues a poor, civilized "bumpkin" while "all hands were in a panic," unable to decide what to do, so that "nothing was done, and nothing seemed capable of being done" [XIII] until Queequeg, with spontaneous grace, acts). In harmony with natural processes, even part *of* them, such men accept nature fully. They have not become estranged from nature by thinking *about* it, as more civilized men have. They may worship nature gods, like Queequeg's benign and familiar Yojo: "a rather good sort of god, who perhaps meant well enough upon the whole, but in all cases did not succeed in his benevolent designs" (XVI), a god so un-awe-inspiring that he can be taken up by Queequeg "very unceremoniously, and bagged . . . in his grego pocket as carelessly as if he were a sportsman bagging a dead woodcock" (III); or they may worship the more powerful and ambiguous sun itself, as Fedallah does. In either case, they feel their gods to be within the natural order, and they accept what the god chooses to grant or deny. Ages ago, perhaps, "in the ghostly aboriginalness of earth's primal generations, when the memory of the first man was a distinct recollection . . . all men his descendants, unknowing whence he came, eyed each other as real phantoms, and asked of the sun and the moon why they were created and to what end" (L); but they have long since stopped asking such questions, because now, to their own satisfaction at least, they *know.* Nature seems to speak to them directly and clearly, as it does among civilized men only to the insane, like Elijah; and therefore they seem able to prophesy, their prophecies ranging from Queequeg's unspectacular greasing of his boat, "working in obedience to some particular presentiment" (LXXXIV) of a whale about to be sighted, to Fedallah's precisely accurate foreknowledge that only hemp could kill Ahab (CXVII). Such men are not afraid of death; they face it as part of nature: for Queequeg, it is no more than a trifle, to be accepted if it is convenient and rejected if it is not (CX), while Fedallah with "fatalistic despair" (CXVIII) persists in what seems to be his mission of betrayal even though he knows it must end in his death. Because they are in tune with processes of nature, men like this impress us as graceful. Their grace is feline and savage, not feminine. Queequeg's gentleness coexistent with his headhunting, and Fedallah's "subtilty" (XLVIII) are as close to female qualities as any of the inhabitants of this masculine world get. Their natural grace allows them to seem part of the rhythms of nature, but it is also a sign of their distance from us, and from the more awkward sailor savages of the Pequod. They are always outside of us; as Queequeg's hieroglyphics, and Queequeg himself, remain "unsolved to the last" (CX), so the white "hair-turbaned

Fedallah remained a muffled mystery to the last" (L). To such men, bits of animate nature, we can never come very close at all.

We can get closer to men like Ishmael, who are less forbiddingly of a piece, who show signs of occasional indecision, and seem rather like ourselves at times. Thus the last major way of encountering the other is also embodied in a fictional technique that reflects a mode of perception. As the book proceeds, the purely comic portraiture loses priority, and the narrator begins to let us overhear private soliloquies, interior conversations less spoken than thought. The other seems much less of an external object to us; it is almost as if we, together with Ishmael (who simply disappears at such points), *become* the other.

But we do so by virtue of a literary convention. And partly because the convention here is noticeably archaic (soliloquies are not "realistic" even in the nineteenth-century romance terms that Melville employs) it calls attention to itself as theatrical; we notice it as a convention—one that forcibly simplifies the complexities of private mental experience. When we "become" the other by means of a soliloquy, we are not in the presence of an unmediated encounter; instead, we remain within the consciousness of a storyteller who *imagines* the other. Thus we break out of solipsism into an inter-subjective world by a technique which maintains the problematic boundaries of selfhood: overtly, the gap between self and other has been bridged, but covertly its eternal existence is acknowledged.

What is revealed of the other by this last method is therefore not inmost, essential selfhood. What is revealed is something like the little lower layer, a stylized, ordered substratum, the revelation of which makes us aware of Ishmael's awareness that an exterior role —Ahab, say, the inflexibly fixed captain bent on revenge—has interior components; and, most typically, that what comprises the interior is self-divided, in process, debating with itself even as it creates masks and roles to conceal its tenuous balances. Thus Starbuck's role of "staid, steadfast man, whose life for the most part was a telling pantomime of action" (XXVI) is revealed in soliloquy to be capable of harboring a consciousness whose "miserable office" is "to obey, rebelling; and worse yet, to hate with touch of pity!" (XXXVIII).

Sometimes Ishmael is willing to go beyond the mere presentation of self-division in order to find abstract, conventional terms for the components of this divided self:

> Starbuck's body and Starbuck's coerced will were Ahab's, so long as Ahab kept his magnet at Starbuck's brain; still he knew that for all this the chief mate, in his soul, abhorred his captain's quest, and could he, would joyfully disintegrate himself from it, or even frustrate it.   [XLVI]

Spirit or soul ("the eternal, living principle" [XLIV] in a man) is here at war with mind or will (the "life-spot" [XLIV] of a man where the spirit resides "leagued with" the mind), which in turn controls body, the outer vessel of the self—these three elements, which may operate together harmoniously as well as discordantly, constitute one schema of total identity for Ishmael.

Of the inwardly discordant characters, Ahab, who outwardly "did long dissemble" (XLI), is of course the major example. When Ishmael analyzes him, he uses terms similar to those he uses to explain Starbuck. An important occasion for analysis is provided by Ahab's behavior during his frequent nightmares, when "a wild cry would be heard through the ship; and with glaring eyes Ahab would burst from his state room" (XLIV). Outwardly the "unappeasedly steadfast hunter of the white whale," inwardly Ahab is torn apart, so that at night

> this Ahab that had gone to his hammock, was not the agent that so caused him to burst from it in horror again. The latter was the eternal, living principle or soul in him; and in sleep, being for the time dissociated from the characterizing mind, which at other times employed it for its outer vehicle or agent, it spontaneously sought escape from the scorching contiguity of

the frantic thing, of which, for the time, it was no longer an integral. But as the mind does not exist unless leagued with the soul, therefore it must have been that, in Ahab's case, yielding up all his thoughts and fancies to his one supreme purpose, that purpose, by its own sheer inveteracy of will, forced itself against gods and devils into a kind of self-assumed, independent being of its own. Nay, could grimly live and burn, while the common vitality to which it was conjoined, fled horror-stricken from the unbidden and unfathered birth. Therefore, the tormented spirit that glared out of bodily eyes, when what seemed Ahab rushed from his room, was for the time but a vacated thing, a formless somnambulistic being, a ray of living light, to be sure, but without an object to color, and therefore a blankness in itself. God help thee, old man, thy thoughts have created a creature in thee; and he whose intense thinking thus makes him a Prometheus; a vulture feeds upon that heart for ever; that vulture the very creature he creates. [XLIV]

The conceptual gist of this difficult passage would seem to be that, when asleep, Ahab's soul, temporarily dissociated from what has insanely used it, rebels. Yet the judiciously analytic Ishmael faced with Ahab's psychic profundities does not simplify his analysis to any such "gist." The passage is full of complex abstractions, qualifications, extensions, synonyms with subtle distinctions implied between them, and second thoughts. Ishmael's first hypothesis is that soul, the eternal, living principle, is dissociated in sleep from Ahab's dominant mind, a mind which in the daytime uses soul for its "outer vehicle or agent." But here Ishmael corrects himself: since mind does not exist apart from soul even in sleep, the first analysis must be wrong. Ishmael tries again: Ahab's mind has created a purpose which at first reflexively characterizes that mind, then itself grows into a discrete entity of monstrous proportions (a vulture feeding upon the heart of its Prometheus-creator) from which flees the "common vitality"—soul plus mind[7]—now animating Ahab's body. The second try, however, is not wholly successful either: it leaves Ahab's "independent purpose" spatially unaccounted for (perhaps a literal-minded quibble, yet the passage does have the air of analytic interpretation as well as of poetry) and it blurs the relation between "common vitality" and "tormented spirit"—presumably one of identity, but we can't be sure—because unstated distinctions seem to be implied. In short, there are loose ends to the precision of Ishmael's analysis; he makes too many abstract synonyms. Indeed, the whole passage, in addition to being susceptible of that kind of exegetical attention it has often received, also shows Ishmael unable to create and revise sufficiently quickly enough static abstractions to keep up with the shifting complexity that is his experience of Ahab. The initially statue-like Ahab of the quarter-deck, "shaped in an unalterable mould, like Cellini's cast Perseus" (XXVIII), his bone leg steadied in an auger hole as if he were a component part of the ship, has here become fragmented almost into incoherence.

Part of what this suggests is that "becoming" the other—becoming, for example, Ahab—by means of soliloquy is more of a deception than my first account of it (on pages 61–62) suggested, for it seems we have become the other only to be able to explain him less convincingly than when he appeared to us as a distanced, animate object, wholly exterior, but at the same time possibly more favorable to the categorial manipulations of the mind—more accessible to thinking about *because* we experienced him as an object. The Ahab of the soliloquies and Ishmael's analyses exists in the duration of time, changing from moment to moment in his secret proportions, and in this moment of nightmare has become "a blankness in itself," a formula which, perversely, seems more adequately descriptive of him even when he is awake than "crazy Ahab" does. The latter is touched with hypocrisy: it pretends to explain Ahab by labeling him, but the label is simply the name that we give to others with whom we can make little or no contact, and therefore can have no real sense of; while the former at least focuses unequivocally on the mystery of Ahab's being. Ahab is a blankness, a whiteness (Ishmael is aware that "blank" means "white" in his usage of it in chapter XLII), with all the ambiguity of that color; but he is also a strange kind of emptiness, a lack, and perhaps a lack in Ishmael's and our rationalizing understanding of him as well as a lack in himself. But how, from our point of view, can a blankness be understood; a being so tormented, so at war with himself; so often at interior variance with his exterior, however much the latter signals the division within; a man, as Ishmael admits near the end (and the sense of which admission has been repeated throughout like a refrain), "every revelation" of whose "deeper part" partakes "more of significant darkness than of explanatory light" (CVI)?

The way in which Ishmael tends to understand Ahab is suggested by the phrase (already cited in context near the end of the quotation on page 63), "without an object to color." Because these words occur soon after the scientific theory (quoted on page 33, above) that earthly colors are not inherent in substances, but are illusions bestowed upon substances by the whiteness of light which itself contains all other colors, what is meant by the phrase is something like this: the mysterious self of Ahab, the mind-soul, is a "ray of living light" which requires for its normal daytime existence an "object to color." Like light, the self contains all possibilities of color, but color other than white can be selectively drawn out of the self's blankness only by its having an object—that is, a goal. The self is here conceived of as a kind of closed circuit between itself and some purpose within itself that can give it normal human character. Since to the Starbuckian triad mind-soul-body must be added object or purpose, and since it is in fact Ahab's willful purpose that characterizes him in his inflexible moods when he is "for ever Ahab," it is Ahab's purpose which is the focus of most of Ishmael's major analyses of him.[8] If Ahab differs from the common run of men chiefly in his sheer *quantity,* in his "greatly superior natural force, with a globular brain and a ponderous heart," all of which adds up to "one in a whole nation's census—a mighty pageant creature, formed for noble tragedies" (XVI); if, as Peleg says, "There's a good deal more of him" (XVI); or, as Elijah says, *"He's* got enough . . . [soul] to make up for all deficiencies of that sort in other chaps" (XIX); then all these quantitative differences come together and achieve definition in the strength of his characterizing purpose. When he is the self-divided Ahab, his purpose momentarily waning, he more obviously "has his humanities" (XVI); he seems more anonymous, more an ordinary fellow creature; it is easier, then, to feel that "all of us are Ahabs" (CXXIII)—but even then, the force of his self-divisions is greater than most men ever experience, and this force points right back to the singular purpose that sets him apart from all men: as Ishmael says, the "symptoms" of his nightmare ambivalence are "but the plainest tokens of . . . [the] intensity" of "his own resolve" (XLIV).

Ahab as the Problematic Other

Ahab's purpose, selectively absorbing a characterizing tonality from the "ray of living light" that is his mind-soul, in turn colors the total Ahab, as well as everything that comes within his view. His major moods are the moods of his purpose, not the passive vagaries of most other men whose mood patterns are less clearly defined. The restful light of early evening is rejected—"This lovely light," he says, "it lights not me" (XXXVII)—because it is out of harmony with his mood-world, a darker, tenser world than Ishmael's. Light for Ahab is restricted to those flames that can match his inner fires: the flaring, ghostly corpusants, the sharp clear blaze of lightning, both leaping momentarily out of darkness.

The effect of his purpose on Ahab's identity can perhaps best be understood against the context of experienced time, which is implied in Ishmael's first sight of him. Ishmael notes the statue-like determination of the body itself, then the whitish rodlike mark that runs down the side of his face and neck and signals the inner self-division, then the posture, "erect, looking straight out beyond the ship's ever-pitching prow" (XXVIII). Captain Ahab's glance, here, is one of total "forward dedication"; for to have such an intense purpose as he has is to live always projected ahead of oneself into the future.

If one has such a purpose, the present does not count at all except as one must live through it in order to allow the future to approach.

When the present intrudes to put off the future, it is impatiently brushed aside:

> Up Burtons and break out? Now that we are nearing Japan; heave-to here for a week to tinker a parcel of old hoops? . . . Begone! Let it leak! [CIX]

To live in the future is to live in the mind, and actuality is displaced to that realm: "What things real are there," asks Ahab, "but imponderable thoughts?" (CXXVII). The merely substantial is despised as mechanical ("D'ye feel brave men, brave?" asks Ahab, and when Stubb responds puppet-like on cue with "As fearless fire," Ahab mutters, "And as mechanical" [CXXXIV]). Yet living with the mind focused on the future nevertheless requires enduring the present, and because the present *is* full of things, like Burtons, and men, like Starbuck, that often seem to impede the future's approach, present substances must be worked upon, molded, coerced, "for be a man's intellectual superiority what it will, it can never assume the practical, available supremacy over other men, without the aid of some sort of external acts and entrenchments, always, in themselves, more or less paltry and base" (XXXIII). The future-living mind is well aware of the baseness of what must be done, but because the future goal is everything, its anticipation colors the present activities so that even tricks like magnetizing a new compass needle with bogus cabalism can give pleasure to one whose quality of mind they would ordinarily be below. Anything in the present that can serve becomes a lever with which to move the future closer. Men are not men, but tools to be manipulated for the sake of the future; carefully, to be sure, because "of all tools used in the shadow of the moon, men are most apt to get out of order" (XLVI). In such enterprises, Ahab is successful: "I thought," he says, "to find one stubborn, at the least; but my one cogged circle fits into all their various wheels, and they revolve" (XXXVI); and he is not wrong in his appraisal of their actions, for they respond to his view of them: "Like machines, they dumbly moved about the decks, ever conscious that the old man's despot eye was on them" (CXXX).

In all such instances, the future, as purpose, has determined the present; and because Ahab's purpose is difficult, if not impossible, to achieve, the present takes on the character of that kind of purpose-future. Substances are hard and sharp, splintered bones and iron lances. Action is sudden, angular, and shot through with the destructively fortuitous. Forces are antagonisms: Zoroastrian dark struggles with light, good with evil, in a power-world in which "the real owner of anything is its commander" (CIX). It is a stern, withholding, father-world rather than a yielding and loving mother-world ("My sweet mother I know not," says Ahab in the fire speech in chapter CXIX); and women have no place in it except to be yearned for in moments when purpose wanes, nor has feminine pity—its purposive emotions are hate, despair, anxiety, and fear.

The Ahab created by Ahab's purpose lives in a world that reflects him. "The firm tower, that is Ahab; the volcano, that is Ahab; the courageous, the undaunted, and virtuous fowl, that, too, is Ahab; all are Ahab; and this round globe is but the image of the rounder globe, which, like a magician's glass, to each and every man in turn but mirrors back his own mysterious self" (XCIV)—here, confronting the doubloon, Ahab speaks for himself and his world; what he says may be true in a subtler, more qualified way for each and every man, but it requires no subtilization to apply to him. He spreads his psyche over all, making the world into *a* world, his world, a coherent universe of certain, dominant physiognomic tone. Others become aspects of him, as well as his tools. In Starbuck he sees, at the end, that part of him which tries to pull him back to home, his memories of wife and child:

> I see my wife and child in thine eye. No, no; stay on board, on board!—lower not when I do; when branded Ahab gives chase to Moby Dick. That hazard shall not be thine. No, no! not with the far away home I see in that eye.   [CXXXII]

Fedallah embodies Ahab's willful purpose in its aspect of self-betrayer, the Narcissus image that stares out of the water-world at him:[9]

Ahab crossed the deck to gaze over on the other side; but started at two reflected, fixed eyes in the water there. Fedallah was motionlessly leaning over the same rail.   [CXXXII]

(Two chapters earlier, Ahab and Fedallah "stood far parted in the starlight; Ahab in his scuttle, the Parsee by the main-mast; but still fixedly gazing upon each other; as if in the Parsee Ahab saw his forethrown shadow, in Ahab the Parsee his abandoned substance" [CXXX]; earlier yet, "Ahab chanced so to stand, that the Parsee occupied his shadow; while, if the Parsee's shadow was there at all it seemed only to blend with, and lengthen Ahab's" [LXXIII].) Pip, like Ahab, is mad, and his madness flees from the same sort of existence that Ahab madly fights. As Ahab is secretly self-divided, other selves within his range of power are divided, even as they carry out his purpose to the point of becoming "one man, not thirty" (CXXXIV), and that man, Ahab.

Material substance often takes on the image of Ahab's purpose in peculiar ways. The Pequod, embarking from Nantucket, "thrusts her vindictive bows into the cold, malicious waves" (XXIII), looking like a whale because she wears "the chased bones of her enemies" (XVI). So much is she a whale, that, "while one sperm whale only fights another sperm whale with his head and jaw . . . he chiefly and contemptuously uses his tail" (LXXXVI) in fights with men and boats; but when Moby Dick sinks the Pequod, he does it the honor of ramming it with "the solid white buttress of his forehead" (CXXXV). Ahab, too, has been made over by his object, as Lewis Mumford first noted, into a queer kind of image of the thing he hunts: Moby Dick has his terrifying white buttress of a forehead— Ahab's brow is so prominent it scares Stubb ("I was so taken all aback with his brow, somehow. It flashed like a bleached bone" [XXIX]); Ahab's leg is cut off—Moby Dick has "three holes punctured in his starboard fluke" (XXXVI); both Ahab and the whale are old. As Ahab and the Pequod both resemble whales, so does Ahab in his thoughts become his boat: "I leave a white and turbid wake," he says, "pale waters, paler cheeks, where'er I sail" (XXXVII); and as the

mates issue "from the cabin with orders so sudden and peremptory
. . . it was plain that they but commanded vicariously" (XXXVIII),
as if Ahab were the Pequod's vitalizing principle.

He did not always have this purpose that can so coerce the matter
of his world, but it is not totally alien to what he once was; rather,
it is a monstrous outgrowth of the early Ahab. The purpose is constantly linked to his willful mind, a mind that, however humanly
insane its premises and conclusions, is nevertheless calculatingly
logical. Even in his

> broad madness, not one jot of his great natural intellect had
> perished. That before living agent, now became the living in-
> strument. If such a furious trope may stand, his special lunacy
> stormed his general sanity, and carried it, and turned all its
> concentrated cannon upon its own mad mark; so that far from
> having lost his strength, Ahab, to that one end, did now possess
> a thousand fold more potency than ever he had sanely brought
> to bear upon any one reasonable object.   [XLI]

His madness has increased his intellectual powers, and does nothing
to prevent his thinking in the terminology of categories and syl-
logisms ("Look ye, pudding-heads should never grant premises"
[CVIII], he advises the carpenter, after having led him to an abstruse
and, from his point of view, absurd conclusion). Typically, his mind
reaches conclusions rigorously based on the premises he is willing to
grant, which are mad ones by ordinary standards. But even the young
Ahab was an intellectual of sorts: "Ahab's been in colleges, as well
as 'mong the cannibals; been used to deeper wonders than the waves
. . ." (XVI), says Peleg; and when Ahab originally went to sea, his
"globular brain . . . [had] by the stillness and seclusion of many long
night-watches in the remotest waters, and beneath constellations
never seen here at the north, been led to think untraditionally and
independently; receiving all nature's sweet or savage impressions
fresh from her own virgin voluntary and confiding breast . . ." (XVI).
Ahab, like Ishmael, has learned about the world from his life at sea,
and intellectualized it.

His mad purpose, then, can be seen as the absurd but nevertheless logical outcome of an argument based upon what his life on the sea has taught him. Like most men, he has generalized his personal experience beyond his special predicament; but unlike most men, he has been willing to draw the most far-reaching conclusions from it, and totally commit himself to them. His madness is in part his intellectual rigor and his insistence on the signification of all things. The argument that supports his insane purpose is most effectively suggested by him in his speech to the corpusants in chapter CXIX. There he acknowledges that the fire-gods are full of "speechless, placeless power," but he asserts that they are not ethical: "To neither love nor reverence wilt thou be kind; and e'en for hate thou canst but kill; and all are killed." Like the God of the Book of Job, they torment good men for their own secret purposes; unlike the Jobean God, they do not cease tormenting until death. "Come in thy lowest form of love," Ahab says, "and I will kneel and kiss thee"; but because Ahab has never had intimations of the gods in this form, he asserts: "Oh, thou clear spirit, of thy fire thou madest me, and like a true child of fire, I breathe it back to thee." Ahab's hate is expressed in irony, here: on the one hand, he suggests that the defiance he proposes reflects the nature of the gods, therefore honors them; on the other hand, he means that the only way a man of integrity can relate to malicious or irresponsible deity is to defy it. The white whale, to Ahab the Leviathan emblem of all gods like these and identified with "all his intellectual and spiritual exasperations" (XLI), must be killed in order to get back at his ultimate tormentors; their "right worship" must be "defiance" to a good man who has seen the dim light. The "darker half" of nature sustains Ahab "with a prouder, if a darker faith" (CXVI).

At this point I should like to digress to the problem of the evaluation of Ahab, who has been weighed by criticism in many different scales. During the 1920s the dominant tendency was to identify Ahab's viewpoint with Melville's (more recent critics—Thompson, for one—sometimes still do this); later, the pendulum swung to relatively simple condemnation of Ahab; while since the '30s most critics, perhaps, have paid at least lip service to some kind of balance of attitudes, usually, however, shifting over to condemnation in the end. Ahab's fire speech illustrates much of the difficulty in evaluating him: the argument implied in it will seem, to a Christian, insane, but to those less committed it can suggest a view of the human condition that has claims of its own to at least metaphorical validity. Everything depends upon whether one is willing to grant Ahab's assumptions, or their emotional bases. *Are* the gods as Ahab describes them, or will there be a reconciliation after death that will reveal the unethical character of much of human experience—that the bad often prosper and the good often fail; that all die, and many innocents die in horrible ways—to have been beside the point? Are human ethics irrelevant to a divine ethic, which supersedes them, and which fallen man can no longer even begin to comprehend? Or, to put the case negatively, do the gods even take notice of man? *Are* there any gods? Ahab has no evidence that any of this is so, and, perhaps hastily (he has after all had fleeting intimations of chaos and atheism: "Sometimes I think there's naught beyond" [XXXVI], he says to Starbuck), Ahab concludes that there *is* no evidence other than what is available to him. On that basis he constructs his insane purpose, and on that basis his ethically monstrous act of sacrificing the Pequod's crew has its own higher ethos.

How can one judge such a man objectively? Starbuck, the law-abiding nominal Christian, finds Ahab "blasphemous" (XXXVI). Stubb, further removed from Christianity, grudgingly approves:

> Well, well; I heard Ahab mutter, "Here some one thrusts these cards into these old hands of mine; swears that I must play them, and no others." And damn me, Ahab, but thou actest right; live in the game, and die it!   [CXVIII]

Ishmael, formerly a Presbyterian but now more liberal in his persuasion, calls Ahab insane; as, ethically, most readers of his book would. Thus the book itself contains a spectrum of judgments, and Ishmael reports them all.

In fact, he incorporates their range. Even as he condemns Ahab, there is something in Ishmael that shares Stubb's reaction. Ishmael calls Ahab mad, yet he says "all mortal greatness is but disease" (XVI), which allows for Ahab's being great. He calls Ahab mad, yet in his account of Pip's madness he suggests that man's insanity may be heaven's sense, which allows, on some unearthly scale of values, for Ahab's being right. This isolates the problem. Father Mapple's sermon, dropping the most discordant elements of its colloquial style, concludes with a peroration that defines the religious hero:

> Delight is to him . . . who against the proud gods and com-
> modores of this earth, ever stands forth his own inexorable self.
> . . . Delight is to him, who gives no quarter in the truth, and
> kills, burns, and destroys all sin though he pluck it out from
> under the robes of Senators and Judges. [IX]

Though, like Ahab's, Father Mapple's God is known to him chiefly by His rod, He is clearly a different God from Ahab's; or, so Ahab might argue, He is the same God, but Mapple has failed to draw the correct conclusions about His nature from what Mapple has himself experienced of that God, as distinct from the stories of Him Mapple has read. To grant the Ahabian argument at least hypothetical status is illuminating, for then the behavior in relation to God that Mapple advocates is (granting Ahab his kind of God) seen to be Ahab's behavior; and it is the behavior of a saint.[10]

It is true that Father Mapple's sermon defines the religious hero in a way which some have held to be inconsistent, but his definition may alternatively be understood as figuring an existential paradox: the story of Jonah demonstrates that religious man must subordinate his own desires to God's will—"if we obey God, we must disobey ourselves"; yet the religious man also, somehow, "stands forth his own inexorable self." The apparent contradiction is perhaps chiefly one of viewpoint: from the outside and from the normal, ethical viewpoint, a saint may look like a self-willed madman; while, subjectively, he may be obeying God. His intensity of insane selfhood may be the sign of his God-possession.[11] The dividing line between saint and madman is often so unclear that it is the long, careful, posthumous process of canonization, not the popular judgment of the moment, that must confer official sanctity. Something of what is implied by the existence of this process far antedates the Catholic Church in the religious category of *trial,* exemplified by the Judaic stories of Abraham and Job.

Within the category of *trial,* as Kierkegaard has explicated it in *Fear and Trembling* and elsewhere, ethical considerations do not obtain because God has teleologically suspended them. If Abraham had followed his ethical promptings and behaved so as prematurely to spare the life of his son Isaac, he would have disobeyed God—his temptation *away* from religious heroism was precisely the normal, humanely *ethical;* Job's ethical justifications before God prove to be beside the point, finally, when God's nonethical "answer" comes. Each religious hero is in a divine trial of the steadfastness of his faith; moreover, it is a trial the very existence of which he cannot be aware of (otherwise not his faith but his prudence would be tested); and within the conditions of which normally ethical behavior could as easily be against the will of God as not. All of which is why, although the ethical and religious spheres may overlap in human existence, they are by no means congruent;[12] and why any contemporary who did not happen to hear the voice of God commanding Abraham must until the last moment of reversal have judged Abraham ethically, and condemned him; and why, even if Ahab were a saint on trial, he must be condemned by Starbuck, Ishmael, and us—for we do not hear the voices.

Precisely this inability to hear seems to be a major point of the fire scene. (Earlier, of course, it is not outside voices that Ahab hears but the ethically perverse voice of his own conscience; yet God may speak in the voice of conscience, too, at least according to the Quakers, and Ahab is a Quaker.) In his dialogue with the fire, Ahab acts out hearing supernatural voices; or, to put it minimally, understanding the message of the flames' vibrations. We do not hear the voices, or know what the flames convey; we hear only Ahab's response to the fire, and must infer for ourselves what the fire says. It is possible that Ahab's performance may be merely opportune showmanship to impress the crew when a fortuitous display of St. Elmo's fire occurs (he has "acted" often enough before for such reasons); or the fire may be god-directed at him, and his responses accurate. We cannot know because, beyond the eeriness of the light of the corpusants, and the appropriateness of its purity to the gods, Ishmael, rather uncharacteristically, gives us no statement or even opinion on the matter. Evidently he does not know. Therefore we are in the exact position of having to judge if a man of obviously great spiritual presence is a heroic madman—here, a fraud in the service of his real madness—or a heroic saint.

And potentially a saint, even though he disobeys the fire-gods; because to their all but overwhelming power he gives "no quarter in the truth." Despite his inner division, like a saint he wills one thing; like Father Mapple's religious hero, Ahab "stands forth his own inexorable self" in that he is willing to kill, burn, and destroy in the name of that possessing vision of truth which he has become, a vision which nevertheless dimly seems to see "some unsuffusing thing beyond" (CXIX) the fire-gods[13] to which all their "eternity is but time" and all their creativeness mechanical—some unsuffusing thing, it should be added, which might be placing Ahab on trial, a trial of the existence of which neither Ishmael nor we nor even Ahab could yet be aware. Like Abraham's, Ahab's temptation away from heroism is the ethical, as Pip and Starbuck embody it.

To sum up the argument thus far, we cannot know that Ahab is religiously wrong. We can simply note that his behavior seems cruel, as when in the name of his total commitment he rejects the plea of the Rachel's captain to help find his son; that such behavior destroys society; and that from the humanly ethical standpoint (the only one which most humans, after all, can take) this must seem wrong, however repeatedly individuals and societies are expendable in a religious context, as evidenced by many Bible stories.

But that the ethical context is not the only one in the book against which to set Ahab is suggested, first, by Ishmael's writing this kind of book about Ahab at all. If Ahab were clearly and only a madman,

there would be no point in presenting him as a kind of hero, meta-
phorically as well as literally *above* other men on his quarter-deck,
a man who *does* more and *says* more, "a Khan of the plank, and a
king of the sea, and a great lord of Leviathans" (XXX),[14] a "mighty
pageant creature, formed for noble tragedies" (XVI). In fact, this
inflated perspective exists in the book more directly presented to us
than the one out of which Ishmael says he created his Ahab, that of
the "poor old whale-hunter" in "all his Nantucket grimness and
shagginess" (XXXIII), which would be all the Ahab the book needed
were he merely to be experienced by us as "crazy Ahab." As it is,
when Ahab speaks with the full force of Melville's power of words,
there is no judging him; his madness becomes like Lear's, transcend-
ing itself along with situation and personality. Why give Ahab such
power? Why let him speak "a bold and nervous lofty language"
(XVI) that creates a Shakespearean atmosphere around him which
provides its own implicit moral perspective on him?[15] Why define
madness as heaven's sense; say that Ahab has "a crucifixion in his
face" (XXVIII); note that in his titanic nightmares "he sleeps with
clenched hands; and wakes with his own bloody nails in his palms"
(XLIV)? Ahab even "in all his fatal pride" (CXXIV) does not
think of himself in quite these terms; the terms, and the evaluations
implied, belong to Ishmael, who, whether he fully means it or not,
does present Ahab as a kind of religious hero. And because he does,
against this implied religious context there can be no question whether
Ahab's passion is true or false; the religion it is in service of may be
true or false, but not the passionate heroism, nor its religious character. Nor does insanity taint the heroism, for if all mortal greatness
is no more than disease, Ahab's insanity, to normally ethical judgment, is the necessary disease of his greatness of passion. Nor does
that insanity disqualify the potential accuracy of Ahab's vision of
evil even to the "reasonable" Ishmael: in a world which at any or all
levels may be divinely or ethically chaotic, ethical madness, religiously manifested, may have its own validity. What, in short, is in question for Ishmael is never the actuality, but the moral value and final
cosmic context, of Ahab's heroism.[16]

To all such presentational evidence may be added the many well-known passages that in relative degrees of directness tend to justify Ahab. There is the passage that advocates the value of glorious death in the service of high and dangerous truths:

> Know ye, now, Bulkington? Glimpses do ye seem to see of that mortally intolerable truth; that all deep, earnest thinking is but the intrepid effort of the soul to keep the open independence of her sea; while the wildest winds of heaven and earth conspire to cast her on the treacherous, slavish shore?
>
> But as in landlessness alone resides the highest truth, shoreless, indefinite as God—so, better is it to perish in that howling infinite, than be ingloriously dashed upon the lee, even if that were safety! ... Terrors of the terrible! is all this agony so vain? ... Up from the spray of thy ocean-perishing—straight up, leaps thy apotheosis!   [XXIII]

(In Ishmael's re-presentation of him, Ahab, too, has been apotheosized.) There is Ishmael's remark on sharks fighting over a dead whale: "If you have never seen that sight, then suspend your decision about the propriety of devil-worship" (LXIV); and Queequeg's summary comment: "Queequeg no care what god made him shark ... wedder Fejee god or Nantucket god; but de god wat made shark must be one dam Ingin" (LXVI). There are, in fact, many more often-quoted passages that could be construed in Ahab's defense; but it seems pointless to rehearse them here.

It is, then, contrary to all such signs of a hidden sympathy for Ahab's outrageous purpose that Ishmael, as narrator, usually maintains an open and direct negative moral estimate of Ahab. Yet, this does not really seem to be a question of a horizontal split between narrator and character, a narrator who admits that the character Ishmael against part of his will got caught up in Ahab's purpose, and who from time to time must reestablish his presence in order to note that fact, and ethically disapprove; but rather a question of a vertical split between aspects of the narrator, who, in retelling, partly relives his life as character, and cannot disavow what he once was.

To some extent he still is what he once was in his attitudes, and does not *want* to disavow these parts of the past and present Ishmael. Because both positive and negative attitudes remain, each must be given weight: on the question of Ahab's final moral status, Ishmael is, though in a more diffuse and hidden sense, as self-divided as Ahab is, and as divided as critics ever since have been.

Ahab's more clearly delineated self-division becomes sharpest near the end of the book. Defined *as* Ahab by his purpose, in chapter CXXXII he becomes momentarily detached from it, and in this lucid interval the gap between his purpose and him is enormous:

> Forty years of continual whaling . . . for forty years to make war on the horrors of the deep! Aye and yes, Starbuck, out of those forty years I have not spent three ashore. When I think of this life I have led; the desolation of solitude it has been. . . . away whole oceans away, from that young girl-wife I wedded past fifty, and sailed for Cape Horn the next day . . .

The speech in context is a long one, an emotional counterpoise to the passion of his goal in that what it says is deeply, agonizingly felt. Then, the "natural," self-regarding part of himself goes on to question why he acts as he does:

> What is it, what nameless, inscrutable, unearthly thing is it; what cozzening, hidden lord and master, and cruel, remorseless emperor commands me; that against all natural lovings and longings, I so keep pushing, and crowding, and jamming myself on all the time; recklessly making me ready to do what in my own proper, natural heart, I durst not so much as dare? Is Ahab, Ahab? Is it I, God, or who, that lifts this arm?

He does not question where his coercive purpose came from in the first place, merely what keeps it so insistently before him. Yet he might have asked that question, too. Originally, his purpose grew within him over a long period:

It is not probable that this monomania in him took its instant rise at the precise time of his bodily dismemberment. Then, in darting at the monster, knife in hand, he had but given loose to a sudden, passionate, corporal animosity; and when he received the stroke that tore him, he probably but felt the agonizing bodily laceration, but nothing more. Yet, when by this collision forced to turn towards home, and for long months of days and weeks, Ahab and anguish lay stretched together in one hammock, rounding in mid winter that dreary, howling Patagonian Cape, then it was, that his torn body and gashed soul bled into one another; and so interfusing, made him mad. That it was only then, on the homeward voyage, after the encounter, that the final monomania seized him, seems all but certain . . .   [XLI]

Forced against his will to return home, bedded and at one with his anguish, enduring the warring elements of the Patagonian Cape, Ahab rebels against this absolute interruption of his freedom. His body and soul bleed into one another to form a unitary maimed being which Ahab, refusing to acknowledge it as himself, passionately disavows. After long weeks of brooding over his condition, he intellectualizes all the elements of the accident, as well as his own present suffering, and the weather, into an emblem of "all his intellectual and spiritual exasperations." It is then that he becomes coldly rational about his purpose; at first, merely reacting against his antagonist in "sudden, passionate, corporal animosity," he has now chosen to become that animosity, and he thereby orders an impulse into a reason for his continued existence. If his exterior fate has required his inmost character for its working out, that character was, originally, no more than a strong tendency to intellectualize into coherent patterns. Beyond this, it was open; yet this was enough to prevent him from experiencing what happened to him as Captain Boomer, for example, of the Samuel Enderby saw *his* encounter with the white whale: the result of awkwardness rather than malice. Ahab's characterizing mind sees malice, which is patterned and

purposive though its purposes may be obscure, rather than awkwardness, which is mere meaningless chance. After his accident, in choosing to live only in relation to it, Ahab has changed its character from
that of a meaningless blow from elemental forces into a chosen
fate. He makes the accident into the central event and meaning of
his life, and thereby retroactively makes himself responsible for what
has happened to him even though he was not at first responsible.
It is as if, in Maurice Blanchot's fine summary phrase, "freedom and
personal impulses much more than the movement of an irresistible
mechanism were the true paths of fatality."[17]

Originally Ahab's purpose came upon him as a choice constructed
out of an impulse and an accident. Now, at the end of the book, he
asks how his purpose can be so irrevocably fixed. He decides in favor
of an exterior fatality, concluding that he is driven by God, by forces
analogous to those of the wind against which he can do nothing.
His decision expresses an emotional paradox: Ahab feels his original
choice was not free, even as he rebels in favor of freedom.

After the moment of tormented self-regard, Ahab's purpose again
takes over, and as it does, his eyes meet Fedallah's reflected in the
water. A short while later his purpose has once more fully become
him and is experienced as "immutably decreed": "Ahab is for ever
Ahab, man. . . . 'Twas rehearsed . . . a billion years before this ocean
rolled" (CXXXIV).

The claims of home upon his "natural" self are put and felt at
their strongest just before their final and total rejection, and Ahab's
death. The gap between self and purpose is made, here, momentarily,
to seem absolute; then, the futurity of purpose suddenly flows into
the present to fill it, and go back "a billion years" besides; it fills
all of time. But this purpose is to become death, and as "all collapsed,
and the great shroud of the sea rolled on as it rolled five thousand
years ago" (CXXXV), the filling of time seems like an emptiness.

Ahab has made his future determine his present, even as he has
made his past (*his* past, chosen by him to be seen in a certain way
out of many potential ways during those weeks of anguished retro-
spection when it flowed through his characterizing mind) determine

his future. Because it is his kind of past that always comes to meet him from his future, he has always lived ahead of himself, *having* no other present but the empty one his future gives him. Even in conversation, he is normally ahead of those with whom he talks, those whose concerns are in the present.[18] The gap, the emptiness, of the end has been there from the moment in which his choice came alive within him. It is as if Ahab's final extreme individualism has been an attempt to put boundaries to the inner lack from which he suffers, even as his individualism creates that lack: in this sense it is that he is at all times "a ray of living light," but also a "blankness." Thus, we, along with Ishmael, encounter Ahab in the book's present, but he "is" always in the future, eluding us. Having the most character of all, Ahab is yet a kind of vacuum, an emptiness, a nothingness; as such we cannot really understand him humanly, and because we cannot, he must seem to us "crazy."

Ishmael's finally inconclusive moral evaluation of Ahab is not separable from his finally inconclusive effort to understand Ahab. With the two exceptions of the comic perspective, which accepts otherness rather than investigate it, and of the vision of love, which is excluded from Ahab's world, Ishmael has tried to understand Ahab by all the means remaining at his disposal: he first saw Ahab as an animate object, then "became" Ahab in soliloquy, then analyzed what he had seen from without and experienced from within. What his extended consideration of Ahab reveals about the Other is at least this: even those who at first seem of a piece—that is, are "characters"—cannot be adequately known; and, partly because they cannot, they cannot be morally judged, even when their behavior seems most strongly to call for such judgment. It is not that to understand is to forgive, but that understanding, condemnation, and forgiveness are all equally impossible without intentionally or unintentionally blinding oneself to part of the evidence.

Ahab has hunted the white whale, and the hunt has been like a hunt for himself, because he *is* the hunt and the purpose of the hunt; and the end of the hunt is death. As Ahab has hunted the whale, so

Ishmael has hunted them both. When Ahab and Moby Dick disappear under the great shroud of the sea, tied to each other in eternal opposition, distorted, Narcissistic mirror images of each other, Ishmael is left behind to ponder his failure to reach the depths with them, and doubtless to give thanks that he has not. But something in him is compelled, like the ancient mariner, to tell the whole long story over and over again, to those who will listen.[19] Each telling is a new attempt to fill the emptiness left by his experience of Ahab and the whale, to fill it with meaning.

5. Time: Causality, Eternity, Death

Time cannot be known apart from what happens in it, and its rates of duration can be experienced best in the tonality of events in time, which determines whether time passes quickly or slowly. Yet time is so much at the heart of what Ishmael seeks to understand that, directly or tangentially, he often speculates about it.

Cause and effect, for example, make plain the serial order and direction of time, so that the quality of the durational time we experience is linked to the way we feel about causality. Are events determined and necessary, are they the product of chance, are they *intended* by the gods or (the obverse of this) by man? If our sense of time passing is dominated by an affirmative answer to one of these questions, the answer colors our prereflective experience of time. In one famous, sanguine passage Ishmael compares time to a loom and himself, weaving a mat with Queequeg, to "a shuttle, mechanically weaving and weaving away at the Fates":

> There lay the fixed threads of the warp subject to but one single, ever returning, unchanging vibration, and that vibration merely enough to admit of the crosswise interblending of other threads with its own. This warp seemed necessity; and here . . . I ply my own shuttle and weave my own destiny into these unalterable threads. Meantime, Queequeg's impulsive, indifferent sword, sometimes hitting the woof slantingly, or crookedly, or strongly, or weakly . . . thus finally shapes both warp and woof; this easy, indifferent sword must be chance—aye, chance, free will, and necessity—no wise incompatible—all interweavingly working together. [XLVII]

The "Loom of Time" happily combines its subordinate elements of chance, necessity, and man's intentions into a causal machine on

which those elements may operate according to their disparate na-
tures. As in this passage Ishmael is not dominated by any one sense
of causality, so his attitude is open, relaxed, and, at the end of the
passage, rather cheerfully complacent. Time itself seems to have
stopped, even as Ishmael seems to have solved the problem of time.
But right here is the flaw: Ishmael's attitude and, in fact, the loom
of idea that grows out of it are themselves the products of a kind of
interregnum *in* time: "a cloudy, sultry afternoon. . . . still and sub-
dued and yet somehow preluding . . . and such an incantation of
revery lurking in the air . . . I say so strange a dreaminess did there
then reign all over the ship and all over the sea . . . that it seemed
as if this were the Loom of Time." The harmonious loom is the appearance of an extraordinary moment. If it is to be an accurate metaphor of the over-all working of causality, at the very least the peaceful complacency in which it is founded must be destroyed; and in
the next moment exactly that happens, as the "preluding" atmosphere
is fulfilled when whales are sighted and the "ball of free will" drops
out of the self-sufficient mechanical pattern as well as out of Ishmael's hand. Evidently the loom may operate under the absolute,
even runaway, dominance of one of its elements—spotting the whale,
Tashtego looks like "some prophet or seer beholding the shadows
of Fate"; and later, in chasing the ultimate whale, the members of
the crew of the Pequod abdicate any sense of their individual freedom, as "all the souls" are "snatched" by "the hand of Fate"
(CXXXIV). In any case, the loom of time, its harmonious elements
in no wise incompatible, can reassure us only for a moment. If time
is a loom, it seems a more sinister loom than Ishmael's account here
suggests, perhaps like that one formed of a whale's skeleton, whereon
"Life folded Death; Death trellised Life; the grim god wived with
youthful Life, and begat him curly-headed glories" (CII).

Whenever Ishmael contemplates time, fatality is the aspect of it
that is most apt to concern him. Like air, the element with which
(in the guise of wind) fate is most often associated (see pages 29–30,
above), fate is a radically elusive component of causality. What

seems at the time it occurs to be freely willed, can disconcert us in
retrospect by seeming to have been fated:

> Though I cannot tell why it was exactly that those stage
> managers, the Fates, put me down for this shabby part of a
> whaling voyage . . . yet, now that I recall all the circumstances,
> I think I can see a little into the springs and motives which
> being cunningly presented to me under various disguises, in-
> duced me to set about performing the part I did, besides cajoling
> me into the delusion that it was a choice resulting from my own
> unbiased freewill and discriminating judgment.   [I]

Yet here in these offhand tones the ultimate question of fate has
been postponed, for what fates Ishmael is his character, not the gods,
as his immediate analysis shows. He got involved on this particular
whaling voyage because "chief among" his motives for going on
any whaling voyage at all "was the overwhelming idea of the great
whale himself," a being both "portentous and mysterious" which
inhabits "wild and distant seas" and is attended by "marvels of a
thousand Patagonian sights and sounds"; all this strangeness can be
a motive for Ishmael because he is "tormented with an everlasting
itch for things remote." Given such an attitude and such a view of
the mysteriousness of the whale, he must needs go whaling; and
when he heads for New Bedford and Nantucket, moved as he is by
an idea of *the strange,* he discovers the strange everywhere, for we
see first of all what we look for. (To give a homely example: if we
go for an aimless walk in the woods, we will see far fewer mushrooms
than if we go on a mushroom-hunting walk.) Ishmael, who intends
to see the strange and exotic—"the actual cannibals . . . chatting at
street corners" (VI)—sees them, although someone else might well
not have been struck with the sight of quite so many "Feegeeans,
Tongatabooarrs, Erromanggoans, Pannangians, and Brighggians" on
the streets of New Bedford. Thus it is no accident that when Queequeg's Yojo "earnestly enjoined that the selection of the ship should
rest wholly with me" (XVI)—Yojo translated by Queequeg is a

very polite god, who doubtless also retires under the bed to put on
his boots—Ishmael's fundamental itch for the remote and the strange
leads him to pick out of the three possibilities available the Pequod,
the only decidedly strange ship there. Even Ishmael's predisposition
to be concerned with omens and portents of the future reflects his
concern with the strange, so that at one point he can explain these as
confirmations of what already exists within the self:

> Ah, ye admonitions and warnings! why stay ye not when ye
> come? But rather are ye predictions than warnings, ye shadows!
> Yet not so much predictions from without, as verifications of
> the foregoing things within. For with little external to con-
> strain us, the innermost necessities in our being, these still drive
> us on.   [XXXVI]

Prophecy, based on such a version of omens, would be possible for
any aspiring seer who can intuit human tendencies: "If you continue
to behave as you do, the following will most likely happen," would
be all that such a seer actually says.[1] The prophet can read "Fate"
because he can read character. If character is fate, according to Ishmael (following Heraclitus), then, in this matter his history serves
to confirm that of Ahab, who also ordered an impulse and a character
tendency into his fate.

But since Ishmael's first analysis of fatality merely suggests that
fate is character working itself out in action, it has postponed the
question of ultimate fatality. Where does character itself come
from? Is it not something imposed, as its etymology suggests, from
without? The true path of fatality may be personal impulse, but the
nature of the impulse does not seem "free" if it cannot be in some
sense chosen; and if fate is to be retained as an operative concept,
surely the gods, or something like them, must have dictated the kind
of impulse likely to appear, if not when it is to appear. Consideration
of the possibility of an irresistible mechanism of godlike forces can
only be postponed, not wholly evaded; for if the universe is to be
experienced as fateful, the forces moving it, whether benign or malignant or escaping those evaluations altogether, must be forces that

intentionally *order;* that, to use Ishmael's ubiquitous word, "pre-destinate."

Whether or not this kind of fatality is abroad in the world is a question that haunts the book. Fate as a variety of necessity assumes some kind of order; order is form; and form is a major part of what is meant by meaning. Philosophically, the ideas of meaning and necessity have always been linked, since meaning can be inherent *in* things only if things are necessary—their meanings guaranteed either by the creator-gods or by a teleology of necessity in nature,[2] the question of the first cause being deferred. If necessity *is* not, then meanings are merely conferred by man according to his concerns and uses for things. In this book, necessity takes the shape of fatality. If there is meaning inherent in the world, in its objects and events, then fatality is possible. But is there meaning in the world?

"Some certain significance," Ishmael asserts at one point (XCIX), "lurks in all things, else all things are little worth, and the round world itself but an empty cipher, except to sell by the cartload, as they do hills about Boston, to fill up some morass in the Milky Way." The statement here is definite: significance lurks *in* things (it is not merely attributed *to* them); meaningful order is present in the world. And yet, this affirmation seems finally equivocal: the dying fall cadence of all the words following "else," which so overbalance the short opening affirmation, seems to embody despair, as if just behind the assertion lurked, like significance, the suspicion that there is no significance in anything. Significance is, or else—the only guarantee offered here for the existence of intrinsic meaning, certain or even uncertain, is the desolation of the alternative; but desolation is too prevalent in Ishmael's world for its absence in this instance to be convincing, to serve as a pledge. If Ishmael would like "significance" to exist (and in his book he is forever amassing not just facts but what he takes their significance to be), something in him at this point is not quite sure that it does. His tenuous doubt is the one more crudely expressed by Flask as a happy positive value when he sees the doubloon's "meaning" as nine hundred and sixty cigars: Flask, too, is part of Ishmael.

As significance would imply order and allow the possibility of fatality, so fatality would certify significance. As Ishmael affirms significance, yet seems unsure of it, so he asserts fatality, yet hedges. His first mention of it is flippant: he says he does not know why he went on this whaling voyage, having always gone to sea before on merchant ships—

> this the invisible police officer of the Fates, who has the constant surveillance of me, and secretly dogs me, and influences me in some unaccountable way—he can better answer that than anyone else. And, doubtless, my going on this whaling voyage, formed part of the grand programme of Providence that was drawn up a long time ago.   [1]

Along with the deflation of (probably) Lear's notion of "God's spies," the absurdity of the Providential program Ishmael then offers

Grand Contested Election for the Presidency
of the United States
Whaling Voyage by One Ishmael
BLOODY BATTLE IN AFFGHANISTAN

—undercuts fatality as a serious concept, here. Only as it is developed along the lines of the fatedness of character and motivation does it lose its flippant tone. In fact, throughout the book Ishmael's references to personal fate are either too easy, an obvious lip service to an ancient idea, or they are serious but subverted. A conspicuous example is the Town-Ho's story, wherein Moby Dick acts as an agent of heavenly justice, Steelkilt has a "fore-ordaining soul," Radney is "predestinated," and Ishmael says things like, "Gentlemen, a strange fatality pervades the whole career of these events, as if verily mapped out before the world itself was charted." References to the idea of fatality come thick and fast, as if this idea were what the story is about. But the references are usually made in what can seem like mock-serious portentousness; and this is a tale told while drinking in a bar, which is itself in Lima, the city of lies and corruption ("you know the proverb all along this coast—'Corrupt as Lima' "); the tale concerns heroic Lakemen and vigorous Erie canallers—surely the comic inflation of the folksong "The Erie Canal" cannot be far away; and, finally, the ethical perfection of the story's incidents excites well-merited disbelief in even its Catholic audience, which ought to have been edified by them:

> " 'Then I entreat you, tell me if to the best of your own conviction, this your story is in substance really true? It is so passing wonderful! Did you get it from an unquestionable source? Bear with me if I seem to press.'
> " 'Also bear with all of us, sir sailor; for we all join in Don Sebastian's suit,' cried the company, with exceeding interest."
>
> [LIV]

The Town-Ho's story is specifically presented *"As Told in the Golden Inn"*—that is, this is only one version of a story of which there are several. It is one that for some reason or other it especially pleases Ishmael to remember, and if we note the open-mouthed response suggested by the just-quoted words, one reason might well be the soul-satisfying (to a storyteller) gullibility of the audience on that occasion. My point is that fatality insisted upon in the context of a lie loses stature.

It is only near the end of the book, when fate is the strength of Ahab's purpose plus its probable outcome, that fatality is not enmeshed in subversion. Yet however often Ishmael in this way betrays his doubts about the idea of fate, at one dramatic level he maintains its possibility. He mocks the unclear prophecies of Elijah ("It is the easiest thing in the world for a man to look as if he had a great secret in him" [XIX]), and explains away the mad prophet, archangel Gabriel, of the Jeroboam ("This terrible event clothed the archangel with added influence; because his credulous disciples believed that he had specifically fore-announced it, instead of only making a general prophecy, which any one might have done, and so chanced to hit one of the many marks in the wide margin allowed,"

LXXI); but in at least two instances he seems to allow precise foreknowledge to stand as that. Because precise acquaintance with the
future could not be possible unless events are fated from without, and
there existed a kind of plan of predestination of which certain men,
close to the forces and gods of nature, could catch glimpses, omens
accurate in detail argue in favor of classic fatality.

The prophecies in question are, first, the one mentioned by Elijah:
"And nothing about his losing his leg last voyage, according to the
prophecy?" (XIX). This is later confirmed by Ahab: "The prophecy
was that I should be dismembered; and—Aye! I lost this leg"
(XXXVII). The second is Fedallah's highly specific prediction, some
elements of which could be merely subtle guesses of the kind already
explained away by Ishmael (e.g. of the "two hearses . . . the visible
wood of the last one must be grown in America," CXVII); but
other elements are too detailed and elaborate to be guesses: the hearse
(Moby Dick himself) "not made by mortal hands"; the fact that
Fedallah must die before Ahab, for although he might kill himself
to fulfill this part of the prediction, he could not then be sure Ahab
would die; then finally, and most specific of all, that hemp alone
would kill Ahab.

If these prophecies stand, then the classic notion of the gods
fating man must also stand. The issue is important for the sort of
world the book finally presents: whether it is finally Ahab's world
or Ishmael's. Because if fatality operates in such particulars—if fatality point by minute point predestinates—then the character of the
predestinating gods as it is evidenced by the ethical nature of their
decrees would go a long way toward supporting the religious and
even ethical correctness of Ahab's defiance of them. They would be
wholly malignant. Their malignancy is what Ahab stakes everything on: he stakes himself on the existence of a coherent but inscrutable malignant *order* decreed by these gods. His despair is that
these father-gods have disposed in some way of his "sweet mother"
(CXIX), a female principle that would have allowed real love in
the world. His hope is that the evil, father fire-gods are not in the
last analysis omnipotent:

> Thou knowest not how came ye, hence callest thyself unbe-
> gotten; certainly knowest not thy beginning, hence callest thy-
> self unbegun. I know that of me, which thou knowest not of
> thyself, oh, thou omnipotent. There is some unsuffusing thing
> beyond thee, thou clear spirit, to whom all thy eternity is but
> time, all thy creativeness mechanical. Through thee, thy flaming
> self, my scorched eyes do dimly see it.   [CXIX]

Ahab's defiance at this point suggests that it is an attempt to break
out of human time; out even of the falsely eternal, actually temporal,
order of the evil gods; and perhaps by so doing to reach the notice
of the all but totally unknown gods beyond them existing in true
eternity. Fedallah's prophecies, and his concomitant function as the
agent of the fire-gods sent to destroy Ahab, do much to substantiate
Ahab's position; for why should the gods go to so much trouble to
get rid of him if they were really omnipotent? Why such cumbersome
plots and risks? What have they to fear from him? Perhaps they are
merely usurpers, like Blake's god of the Tyger. Perhaps not only is
Ahab religiously and ethically right to defy them, but if he could
break through to whatever lies beyond them, perhaps there would
be new hope for all men—perhaps Ahab *is* a Christ, even as his
self-crucifying nails suggest.

But finally it is Ishmael's world that the book presents: a world
that includes Ahab's and acknowledges the hypothetical validity of
Ahab's view of things, though it is not committed to that view. The
clear certainty of the precise prophecies is subverted—not in the
sense that Fedallah is a mad but shrewd faker, unmotivated beyond
this, willing to kill himself to ensure the correctness of his forecast
and able to guess, given the nature of the whale line as Ishmael
describes it in chapter LX,[3] and given the nature of Ahab's habits
in his whale boat, that Ahab's own whale rope would be the most
probable source of his death. The subversion of these prophecies
seems, in part, more a matter of point of view. Ishmael confirms
Elijah's report of a prediction that Ahab would lose his leg in a
soliloquy of Ahab's, delivered within his cabin, *"sitting alone"* (the

italicized words are part of the stage directions for chapter XXXVII): Ishmael could not have heard the confirmation. Similarly, the conversation between Ahab and Fedallah takes place in Ahab's whale boat while they keep vigil over a dead whale at a time long before Ishmael became a member of that boat crew[4] and could have overheard it. These prophecies and their confirmation are elements that Ishmael has added to the "facts" of his story, to that actuality to which he could personally bear witness. He has added them either on the basis of hearsay or out of pure invention, since he could never have been certain of their truth.

His reasons for adding the prophecies to what he could know of the facts are meaningful if we remember that it is *Ishmael* and not Melville who "writes" this book; that Ishmael has all along characterized himself as a storyteller; and that his reasons for telling his story in this manner with these Gothicisms may therefore help characterize *his* predicament as writer and storyteller rather than Melville's (whose use of such prophecies could well be explained by his unfortunate—in this instance—fondness for Shakespeare). Thus, of the prophecies or their detailed working-out, Ishmael could not have been certain; what at the time of the story's events he *was* certain of was that Ahab was sure enough of his view of things to act out the terrible fate that increasingly became his own. As an actual member of the Pequod's crew, Ishmael sensed greatness as well as madness in Ahab. As a storyteller, he must make his sense of that greatness plausible: he must use his conventional license as storyteller to ensure more than a "crazy Ahab" status for his hero. Yet he cannot simply underwrite Ahab's view of things and also maintain the doubleness of his own view. What he does is imagine the highly specific prophecies in strict relation to Ahab's intensity of purpose— that is, in relation to what Ahab's chief mode of being is. The sign of this is that the prophecies exist in the book literally only in intimate conjunction with Ahab: the one prophecy, confirmed in his soliloquizing mind when he is alone; the other, brought into being by Fedallah, the external mirror of Ahab's purpose. Part of Ahab's world, they help define its nature and thereby define the nature of

Ahab's heroism. For those who are not Ahabs and have no Fedallahs, the prophecies need not be "real."

Thus, in this matter as in all his other attempts to contemplate or explain fatality, Ishmael reaches no final conviction. He is attracted to the idea of fatality enough to let it stand within Ahab's realm of influence, to image that realm with all the traditional apparatus surrounding a tragic hero; but he is unsure enough of it to adopt it for himself, now outside of Ahab's realm, only with playfulness and subversion. Here he is partially a victim of his temporal perspective: the events he sees under the aspect of fate took place in his past, and the sense of fatality, whatever else it is, is a function of hindsight. Events locked into the form of a coherent story that is over when it is told must seem fated because the end is known, and it has followed from the beginning: it is only "now that I recall all the circumstances" (I) that they do seem fated to Ishmael; it is only when Ahab admits to himself the probable end of the pattern of his action that he says the "act's immutably decreed" (CXXXIV). But life is lived forward in an eternal present without benefit of the hindsight that is Ishmael's at the start of his story; and, whether in actuality fated or not, the eternal present must be experienced, as Dr. Johnson knew, as at least potentially free, for even when we say we cannot do otherwise, we know that we can: that the impulse to do otherwise might at any moment arise, and that if it did, we might just obey it; or we might not. Ishmael's basic indecision about fatality is further related to a certain shiftiness in his temporal stance: he tells a story, but in telling it he relives its events, making (for us and for himself) his personal past into a kind of present. Sometimes, however, especially in the analytic passages, the presentness of this past clearly becomes a pastness again: less immediate, more distanced in that it is now unequivocally the object of his reflections. Sometimes, the relative presentness of the recreated past becomes pure present, as in the episodes that are all dialogue, or in breathless accounts of pre-reflective action. Such movement of events closer and further away in time as Ishmael tells them has a function within his efforts to vary his perspectives on his material in order to understand it: "But you must look at this matter in every light" (CX), he says repeatedly—"But look at this matter in other lights; weigh it in all sorts of scales" (XXIV); "But as you come nearer to this . . . it begins to assume different aspects, according to your point of view" (LXXV). He tries in this way to comprehend his past, for sometimes present immediacy will be more successful cognitively than distance and analysis will. But along with this gain in intellectual shiftiness and in the accuracy with which the total situation of "telling a story about the past" is denoted, goes a loss in the simplicity and decisiveness which could make fatality seem either true or untrue. Consequently, it must seem both. If the idea of predestination is to Stubb an "unfailing comfort" (XXXIX) because it allows him to ask no questions, and to Ahab an outrage because it seems to him reductive of human dignity,[5] to Ishmael—the insistent questioner who does not believe that appearances are an index to dignity[6]—predestination is wholly ambivalent. Able to neither accept nor reject, yet finding the issue important, Ishmael, as usual, has it both ways.

Predestination is one more unsolved mystery in the long catalogue of the strange and fantastic, elements of which continually erupt into the everyday when the land world is replaced by the sea world, a realm in which matters are so often incomprehensible that no sense of normal reality can be located in anything that occupies space. Similarly, because of predestination no such reality can be located in time. If, for example, fatality were certain, then those events that are predestined would be more "real" (in the Platonic sense) at the time of predestination, which is to say in God's time—eternity; for time itself "began with man" (CIV). Just as Ishmael suspects that everything may be secretly *white* but cannot be sure of this, so he does not know the temporal condition of reality. Given his drive toward the potential reality of the strange and the distant, and his edgy concern with predestination, his interest in the subject of eternity could not but be pervasive.

Pervasive, but not as often out in the open. Causality, fate, neces-

sity, predestination: these are abstractions, but whatever they stand
for can to some degree be experienced in time, while alive. Eternity,
like death, is the pure abstract; about both, there are fewer things
Ishmael can say. Nevertheless, the idea of eternity seems to constitute
a large part of his apprehensive attention to whales, and in this
respect pervades his book. Portentous and mysterious, these creatures
at the outset dualistically, "two and two," float imaginatively into
his inmost soul in "endless procession" (I)—the durational adjective
immediately suggests the special relationship whales have to time.
Because the "Sperm Whale blows as a clock ticks, with the same
undeviating and reliable uniformity" (XLVII), the whale is a kind
of living clock; but also, says Ishmael, "I am horror-struck at this
ante-mosaic, unsourced existence of the unspeakable terrors of the
whale, which, having been before all time, must needs exist after
all humane ages are over" (CIV). Itself incarnating time, the whale
outspans the limits of time; or, more accurately, "we account the
whale immortal in his species, however perishable in his individual-
ity" (CV). The whale exists in time, but the idea of whales suggests
the impingement of eternity on time.

Thus Moby Dick, who in his whiteness contains (like white light)
all the possible tonalities of whaledom, is rumored to be "not only
ubiquitous, but immortal (for immortality is but ubiquity in time)"
(XLI); and at the end it is his head which is "predestinating"
(CXXXV) and causes death. As the Pequod approaches him, "Time
itself now held long breaths with keen suspense" (CXXXV). Evidently, to know this ultimate whale would be to have insight into
eternity: potentially, at least, the realm of the most real.

Death, the end of time for living creatures, is also a compelling
subject for Ishmael. "There is," he says, "death in this business of
whaling—a speechlessly quick chaotic bundling of a man into
Eternity" (VII). Sailors are always "tinkering at their last wills and
testaments" (XLIX). Though they become familiar with death
around them, and must treat it as an everyday part of their life, the
degree of ease with which they actually confront it depends upon

the extent to which they are savages (Queequeg's stately acceptance and then rejection of his impending death surprises even the savage crew of the Pequod), or upon the quality of their imaginations (Stubb and Flask are more casual about it than Starbuck). For the highly imaginative Ishmael, death never loses its original awefulness and attraction.

If time is the becoming of Being, death is the futureward direction of time: it is an eternity wherein (from living man's viewpoint) Being seems static, and may be finally knowable, as the frequent links between profundity, truth, and death suggest (see pages 39–41, above). When he goes to sea as a "substitute for pistol and ball" (I), Ishmael does so as an alternative to death, but it proves to be an ambiguous one, because, although travel and motion are part of the processional character of life, Ishmael also finds it possible to imagine death as a mysterious continuation of life's journey: as "a launching into the region of the strange Untried; it is but the first salutation to the possibilities of the immense Remote, the Wild, the Watery, the Unshored" (CXIII). The original choice of going to sea involves an assertion of life by the risking, even courting, of death. It is associated with intellectual ambivalence, perhaps even with intellectual contradiction: "With a philosophical flourish Cato throws himself upon his sword," says Ishmael; "I quietly take to the ship" (I).[7] The original ambivalence or contradiction persists emotionally as a kind of sympathetic antipathy. His first extended meditation on death (while awaiting the appearance of Father Mapple) swings alternately between horror at the idea of "eternal, unstirring paralysis" (VII) and almost anticipatory joy at the idea of immortality.[8] Clearly, he is fascinated by death: he notes that the eyes of the temporarily dying Queequeg

> seemed rounding and rounding, like the rings of Eternity. An awe that cannot be named would steal over you as you sat by the side of this waning savage, and saw as strange things in his face, as any beheld who were bystanders when Zoroaster died. For whatever is truly wondrous and fearful in man, never yet

was put into words or books. And the drawing near of Death, which alike levels all, alike impresses all with a last revelation, which only an author from the dead could adequately tell. [CX]

Ishmael has here gotten close to death, but all he can record is how its drawing near looks. Whatever absolute truth may be contained in the eternity to which death is the gateway he cannot tell, because he lives in time.

Time: Duration

Man moves forward in time toward his own possibilities. The flow of time is his ground; or, rather, he *is* time, and the way he incarnates it sums him up: what he was, is, and will be. To understand time would be to understand earthly Being, which is becoming; to understand one's own time would be to understand oneself.

Much more adequately than he can tell us about death and eternity, Ishmael can tell us what it feels like to live in time. It can be exhilarating. All of time is Ishmael's province. From his standpoint in the present, he moves between the most up-to-date scientific authorities and the most ancient historians. Nothing escapes his scholarship. He takes an obvious joy in the range of his ideas and references. But mentally to inhabit all of historical time like this is not really to master it, as Ishmael is often aware. To know history is merely to know historians, who are suspect. Not only the accuracy of the Bible suffers (in the matter of Jonah, when confronted with the common-sense objections of "one old Sag-Harbor whaleman," LXXXIII), but also that of other revered authorities proves vulnerable. Procopius, for example, we are told, "has always been considered a most trustworthy and unexaggerating historian, except in one or two particulars, not at all affecting the matter presently to be mentioned" (XLV), but Ishmael's assurances here are suspiciously offhand and hasty. Later, in chapter CV, because Ishmael does not agree with them, Pliny as well as more recent authorities like Lacépède are brushed aside in order to accept the word of one "Harto, the historian of Goa."

The story of Hercules and the whale is considered "by the best contradictory authorities . . . to be derived from the still more ancient Hebrew story of Jonah and the whale; and vice versa; certainly they are very similar" (LXXXII). Because the best historians most contradict each other, knowledge of the historical past is limited to choosing the historian whose version of what happened you like best. As for the future, precise knowledge of that is limited to omens: "Coffin?—Spouter?—Rather ominous in that particular connexion, thought I" (II), an omen later compounded:

> A Coffin my innkeeper upon landing in my first whaling port; tombstones staring at me in the whaleman's chapel; and here a gallows! and a pair of prodigious black pots too! Are these last throwing out oblique hints touching Tophet?   [XV]

Such degraded omens of the future as come directly to Ishmael point only toward death; but to know that about the future, no omens are necessary.

With the "real" past and future ultimately inaccessible, one is caught in the present, in existential time, where the character of experience is a "universal thump" (I); and "hardly have we mortals by long toilings extracted from this world's bulk its small but valuable sperm . . . when . . . away we sail again" (XCVIII); and "there is no steady unretracing progress in this life; we do not advance through fixed gradations and at the last one pause" (CXIV). The present is a present of repetitive everyday tasks; man lives through an eternal now that takes the serial form of stages, but he is never to rest in any "pondering repose," even "of If" (CXIV). Under this aspect, history itself, however unknowable in detail it may be, must take on the character of the present: the character of repetition, even in its most extraordinary events, for "all marvels," says Ishmael, "are mere repetitions of the ages; so that for the millionth time we say amen with Solomon—Verily there is nothing new under the sun" (XLV).

Under this aspect, predestination, if it exists, becomes a kind of metempsychosis: "Oh! Pythagoras, that in bright Greece, two thousand years ago, did die, so good, so wise, so mild; I sailed with thee along the Peruvian coast last voyage—and, foolish as I am, taught thee, a green simple boy, how to splice a rope" (XCVIII). Predestination is thus in the first place an infinite regress, like Ahab's gods dimly seen behind the fire-gods: sometime in eternity, earthly events may have been fated, but once fated, they were condemned to repeat themselves. Because the shape of coming events is not often predictable in detail, *rigorous* fatality remains an uncertain idea; but granting events many variations within their cycles, they can recur as permanent possibilities of human existence. Ahab's and Ishmael's story redefines and interconnects as it repeats the stories of their namesake predecessors; the present brings the past to life only by re-exploring its potential. It is out of his feeling for such repetition and variation that Ishmael the storyteller names himself Ishmael, and Ahab (probably) Ahab.[9] This is one basic sense in which all historical time is experienceable as a *now.*

But to live an eternally repetitive present is also to feel locked up in time. Standing on board " 'the Moss,' the little Nantucket packet schooner" as "it glided down the Acushnet river," Ishmael once more describes the constricting present:

> On one side, New Bedford rose in terraces of streets, their ice-covered trees all glittering in the clear, cold air. Huge hills and mountains of casks on casks were piled upon her wharves, and side by side the world-wandering whale ships lay silent and safely moored at last; while from others came a sound of carpenters and coopers, with blended noises of fires and forges to melt the pitch, all betokening that new cruises were on the start; that one most perilous and long voyage ended, only begins a second; and a second ended, only begins a third, and so on, for ever and for aye. Such is the endlessness, yea, the intolerableness of all earthly effort.   [XIII]

It is from this repetitive present that Ishmael seeks to escape by going to sea:

> Gaining the more open water, the bracing breeze waxed fresh; the little Moss tossed the quick foam from her bow, as a young colt his snortings. How I snuffed that Tartar air!—how I spurned that turnpike earth!—that common highway all over dented with the marks of slavish heels and hoofs; and turned me to admire the magnanimity of the sea which will permit no records.   [XIII]

To permit records is to allow the recording of history's eternal round, which is what Ishmael tries to get out of. The extravagant rhetoric here is, as usual, a clue to the doom of these particular hopes, for life at sea will prove to be, like land life, an endless routine, differing from that of land only in that it accommodates more wonders; but in a whaler wonders soon wane by their very repetition.

Because the character Ishmael does not yet know this, the narrator re-presents his beginnings as hopefully oriented toward the future, living in glad anticipation. Like Ahab, Ishmael tries by going to sea to reinvent his future by willing a change in its patterned character. His ascents to the masthead are as much attempts to get out of time as to get out of circular movement; the inviting vortex leads to eternity as well as to restful stasis. Ishmael makes his will, he says, for "the fourth time in my nautical career" on this voyage, so that

> all the days I should now live would be as good as the days that Lazarus lived after his resurrection; a supplementary clean gain of so many months or weeks as the case might be. I survived myself; my death and burial were locked up in my chest. I looked round me tranquilly and contentedly, like a quiet ghost with a clean conscience sitting inside the bars of a snug family vault.   [XLIX]

To survive oneself by breaking out of time into eternity is Ishmael's initial goal. But time in its infinite repetition is itself a kind of degraded eternity. Going to sea on a whaler involves not only routine but horizontal movement over the "terraqueous globe" in pursuit of "the circus-running sun" that races "within his fiery ring, and needs no sustenance but what's in himself" (LXXXVII). Ishmael follows that sun westward into the future which seemed so promisingly new and strange at the beginning, only to find that the future resembles the past and west becomes east: "The way behind," says Georges Poulet, "will suddenly take the place of the way ahead"[10] as, with a series of reversals, even the ultimate whale is approached.

The circular character of time is implied first of all by its basis in a spatial analogy: clock time is the moving of a hand through three hundred and sixty degrees of arc in twelve steps. More distantly, the stars revolve in the sky, creating experienced time in the circularity of the seasons. For Ishmael this means that past and future are knowable chiefly as analogues of the present. The past is never other than what has happened as it appears now, in this moment, in this mood; the future is this presentative past that Ishmael throws forward in time: it is what will come as it comes to meet him now. Because the future is full of the past, it means to Ishmael that the future can be experienced either as a repetitive emptiness, as Peleg unknowingly implies when he asks Ishmael what the water-world looks like (XVI),[11] or as a fullness, as Ishmael continues to insist against that part of himself which agrees with Peleg.

Ishmael would like to escape endless circularity. A final vertical movement, he hopes at certain points, would free him; but throughout the book he remains caught in the horizontality of time. He plays the temporal man, to Ahab's man of eternity. His attempt to fill the emptiness of his experience of Ahab and the whale is finally an attempt to give meaning to all of time.

6. ISHMAEL

WHAT THIS CHAPTER will try to demonstrate is that Ishmael's overt character and history are consistent with his emotions, which in turn constitute his universe of space, time, body, and others; and that that universe is totally coherent, even if it occasionally seems not to be.

Ishmael is "of a broad-shouldered make" (XVI), presumably in his twenties when he voyages with Ahab. He is both practical ("I always go to sea as a sailor, because they make a point of paying me for my trouble," I) and a dreamer ("With the problem of the universe revolving in me, how could I—being left completely to myself at such a thought-engendering altitude—how could I but lightly hold my obligations to . . . 'Keep your weather eye open, and sing out every time,' " XXXV). Though his need to support himself has driven him to take various jobs—he has "been a stone-mason, and also a great digger of ditches, canals, and wells, wine-vaults, cellars, and cisterns of all sorts" (CIV), as well as a "country schoolmaster" (I)—their number and diversity testify to a certain irresponsibility that takes no pride in being conventional:

> For my part, I abominate all honorable respectable toils, trials, and tribulations of every kind whatsoever. It is quite as much as I can do to take care of myself, without taking care of ships, barques, brigs, schooners, and what not.   [I]

Insofar as Ishmael has reached any occupational stability at all, it is in his final choice of job: ordinary seaman. Before sailing on the Pequod, he "had been four voyages in the merchant" (XVI) marine (on which voyages he had made his will three times, XLIX). Despite his various bits of advice to the reader to embrace the land values of marriage, stability,[1] and so on, he never follows that advice himself, since at the time he tells his story to us he remains a sailor ("When-

ever I find myself growing grim . . . I account it high time to get to
sea as soon as I can," he says, not: "Whenever I found . . . I accounted"). That he remains a sailor even after his disastrous trip on
the Pequod is further evidenced at the end of the Town-Ho's story:
"I have seen," he says, "and talked with Steelkilt since the death of
Radney" (LIV), "I trod the ship; I knew the crew," a conversation
only possible on a voyage subsequent to the Pequod's. Though this
evidence may be suspect because of its context and purpose, as may
be Ishmael's account of a whale that he hunted twice in three years
(XLV), his report of the "fine gam" he had aboard the Samuel
Enderby "long, very long after old Ahab touched her planks with
his ivory heel" (CI) is not. Similarly, he has not followed his own
advice on marriage, either:

> How it is I know not; but there is no place like a bed for confi-
> dential disclosures between friends. Man and wife, *they say*
> [italics added], there open the very bottoms of their souls to
> each other . . .   [x]

Evidently, his "itch for things remote" (I) governs his practicality,
since it dictates both the variety of his jobs and the final choice of
wandering. Though he is driven to seek the strange, and is "quick
to perceive a horror," he "could still be social with it" (I), if allowed
to be. Being social with horrors means several things, among them
simple acceptance, through love, as with Queequeg; intense, unmediated confrontation, as with the giant squid (LIX); endless speculation about the causes of horror in the world; endless presentation
of all that can be known about the cannibal state of nature. The last
two socialities dominate the book, for though Ishmael would like to
be social, he also likes to understand. Ignorance, the parent of fear,
disturbs him; if, unlike Ahab, he does not "hate" the "inscrutable
thing" (XXXVI), inscrutability bothers him enough to make him
devote much time and energy to looking up *facts,* as well as in all
probability influencing his temporary vocation (just before becoming a sailor) of schoolteacher.

Governed by his itch for socializing with the remote, Ishmael has left the heritage of his family, which is an "old established" one "in the land" (I). Though he perhaps got the idea of going to sea from the example of an uncle of his, a certain "Captain D'Wolf ... who, after a long life of unusual adventures as a sea-captain, this day resides in the village of Dorchester, near Boston" (XLV), he does not follow his uncle's example in aspiring to either captaincy or secluded retirement. The detailed sketchiness of his more or less patrician family history raises some questions the book apparently does not try to answer. Why did Ishmael leave home? If the family fortunes had suffered a change, why did he reject part of his uncle's example while accepting the rest? Why didn't he get work suited to his background and education? Why does he seek out the strange?

About such matters little is directly said, but there are several clues. There is, for example, no mention of a father; only a stepmother, who "was all the time whipping me, or sending me to bed supperless" (IV). Ishmael left home because, where there is no love, one is already emotionally homeless. Answers to the other questions might best be approached by a close analysis of what going to sea in the style and for the reason that he does means to him emotionally; and connecting that analysis with the character of his emotionally homeless past.

"Whenever," Ishmael says, "I find myself growing grim about the mouth; whenever it is a damp, drizzly November in my soul . . . then, I account it high time to get to sea as soon as I can." In this recurrent mood, land life seems bleakly constricting: men are "tied to counters, nailed to benches, clinched to desks." In the face of such constriction, one must feel restlessly aggressive: "it requires a strong moral principle to prevent me from deliberately stepping into the street, and methodically knocking people's hats off." Land life is a kind of living death, so that Ishmael finds himself "involuntarily pausing before coffin warehouses, and bringing up the rear of every funeral" that he meets, as if by the contrast to reassure himself that he still lives. His going to sea is a "substitute for pistol and ball," as if uninterrupted land life would drive him to suicide, an act which merges the desires passively to die, actively to destroy oneself, and even more actively to obliterate the surrounding intolerable world itself; and though suicide is not offered by Ishmael as a real possibility for himself, its being jokingly mentioned points the directions of his recurrent emotion. He is bored, achingly so. In his mood, land life can offer "nothing particular to interest" him, so that on land there is nothing able to channel the aggressive restlessness which his experience of bleak constriction generates.

Boredom is a dialectical emotion. It is in the first place a perception of meaninglessness around one and within one. To be bored is literally to be hollowed out, and to experience hollowness.[2] In Ishmael's case there is nothing particular to do because there is everything to do, but nothing offers itself as worth doing. Because the world is empty, its very freedom is experienced as constriction. The future is blocked; the present stretches, and mockingly lingers. One is caught in time, just as one is caught in space, and in the perverse, inert thingness of objects. In this spatial and temporal prison any action becomes a flight from inaction. There is a strong urge somehow to break out of one's own world, perhaps aggressively to connect with that of another, or simply to break out by talking with someone (*Moby Dick* begins and ends in loneliness). Because the inert, meaningless emptiness of shapes, events, people, and time is intolerable, it invites filling up: "the interesting" becomes the governing category of life. The more exotic something is, the better chance it has of forcing entry into a bored consciousness, as if it had an intenser reality that could overcome the poisonously uniform unreality of the daily round.

This is why Ishmael's analysis of his antidote to the bleak November in his soul begins with daydreams and reveries, intimations of the interesting. Compared with land, the sea, he argues, in giving rise to these revivifying intimations, is "magic," full of "charm," even "holy." Miraculously, it can compel full attention. Miraculously, it can generate interest. Having no stultifying boundaries, it seems a mental realm of sheer openness; if boredom is an unacceptable freedom, the sea offers acceptable freedom in the guise of the strange, the adventurous, the wonderful. One must go to sea as an ordinary

sailor in simple harmony with this aspect of it, for although all men
are slaves, men with responsibilities for entire "ships, barques, brigs,
schooners" are everlasting slaves to the duties entailed by their "glory
and distinction." Sailors can steal more and headier moments of freedom than either captains or cooks, who might as well have never
left land.

The idea of recurrent boredom, then, can answer all the questions
asked about why Ishmael goes to sea as an ordinary sailor, despite his
patrician background: he seeks the freedom of the strange. But why
is he recurrently bored? Or, to put it more accurately and less pejora-
tively, why does the perception of the universal emptiness of self and
world that boredom implies overwhelm him from time to time?

In describing some of his initial feelings about Queequeg, the
horror he becomes most social with, Ishmael recounts at some length
an extraordinary waking-dream he once had as a child. Before it
came to him, his stepmother had punished him for "cutting up some
caper or other" (IV): she had "dragged me by the legs . . . and pushed
me off to bed, though it was only two in the afternoon of . . . the
longest day of the year in our hemisphere"—literally, the 21st day
of June; figuratively, the stretching out of the hours of that day:

> . . . up stairs I went to my little room in the third floor, undressed
> myself as slowly as possible so as to kill time, and with a bitter
> sigh got between the sheets.
>
> I lay there dismally calculating that sixteen entire hours must
> elapse before I could hope for a resurrection. Sixteen hours in
> bed! the small of my back ached to think of it.

Duration has become eternal in its emptiness. Time must be killed
because its freedom is useless, oppressive. The childhood experience
of boredom is like a death from which one hopes hopelessly for a
resurrection.

> And it was so light too; the sun shining in at the window, and
> a great rattling of coaches in the streets, and the sound of gay
> voices all over the house. I felt worse and worse—

Mockingly surrounded by the normal, happily purposive daytime world, Ishmael can stand the isolation of boredom no longer, and tries to break out of his prison, to make contact again with ordinary reality:

> at last I got up, dressed, and softly going down in my stockinged feet, sought out my stepmother, and suddenly threw myself at her feet, beseeching her as a particular favor to give me a good slippering for my misbehavior; anything indeed but condemning me to lie abed such an unendurable length of time. But she was the best and most conscientious of stepmothers, and back I had to go to my room.

The apparent sentimentality of Ishmael's lingering account of this childhood episode is a sign of its content. What he asks from his stepmother is not just a beating but an evidence of her human concern for him. Her sending him away to get him out of her sight negates his existence for her, and in some dim way he understands that. A beating would require her and his emotional presence; it would be a token of her love; and love is what would have given him a home in the normal, sunlit world. But she forces him to return to the emptiness of the time and space of his room. She makes *that* his reality, and decades later it remains an overwhelming one:

> For several hours I lay there broad awake, feeling a great deal worse than I have ever done since, *even from the greatest subsequent misfortunes* [italics added]. At last I must have fallen into a troubled nightmare of a doze; and slowly waking from it—half steeped in dreams—I opened my eyes, and the before sun-lit room was now wrapped in outer darkness. Instantly I felt a shock running through all my frame; nothing was to be seen, and nothing was to be heard; but a supernatural hand seemed placed in mine. My arm hung over the counterpane, and the nameless, unimaginable, silent form or phantom, to which the hand belonged, seemed closely seated by my bedside. For what seemed ages piled on ages, I lay there, frozen with

the most awful fears, not daring to drag away my hand; yet
ever thinking that if I could but stir it one single inch, the
horrid spell would be broken. I knew not how this consciousness
at last glided away from me; but waking in the morning, I
shudderingly remembered it all, and for days and weeks and
months afterwards I lost myself in confounding attempts to
explain the mystery. Nay, to this very hour, I often puzzle myself with it.

Rejected by his stepmother, Ishmael has been put outside the world
of normal, everyday reality. When out of the darkness, although
"nothing was to be seen, and nothing was to be heard," comes "a
supernatural hand" to take his, it is as if Nothingness itself—the
nameless, the unimaginable, the silent—has come to claim Ishmael
for its child. Perhaps it seeks to comfort him, or merely to confirm
his restriction and exile; either could be the case, for the naught does
not speak. But in either case, it comes to him *personally,* decisively,
in a form that can never be explained away, though his second and
continuing reaction to his primal experience of this inmost essence
of the strange is to try.[3]
    Years later, when his habit of explanation is quite settled, he uses
his dream to describe what it felt like to wake up and find a cannibal's
arm around him in bed:

> Now, take away the awful fear, and my sensations at feeling
> the supernatural hand in mine were very similar, in their
> strangeness, to those which I experienced on waking up and
> seeing Queequeg's pagan arm thrown around me. But at length
> all the past night's events soberly recurred, one by one, in fixed
> reality, and then I lay only alive to the comical predicament.

Between childhood and maturity, Ishmael has grown relatively comfortable with the idea of the strange. He still tries to explain it, but
in a more easygoing fashion. Its total wonder has diminished. But
at the time that the inexplicable first accepted him for its own, what

he felt (whatever the intentions of the supernatural hand) was not comfort, but fear.

"Awful fear": the adjective retains its original force. Fear and awe make a particular kind of fear. It is not fear against which anything can be done; although thinking that if he could only move his hand "one single inch, the horrid spell would be broken," Ishmael does not do so. The hand makes no threatening move; it does nothing but rest in his. It is merely *there,* against all reason. In that moment of experiencing its presence, however long or short a moment it may have been as measured by the clock, all of time is blocked; Ishmael cannot stir to break time's interminable emptiness. Time is "ages piled on ages," as if his anterior boredom, itself already having had all the intensity that youthful boredom can have, had been raised to the power of dread.

Like boredom, dread is an encounter with emptiness, but an authentic, unmediated encounter. The naught is faced in utter loneliness. There is no possibility of evasion. As Kierkegaard has made notoriously clear, *Angst,* whether experienced intensely as dread or diffusely as anxiety, is a kind of apprehension of the future, a something which is yet "nothing." At the level of dread, it is indecisive fear without a tangible object: something about the immediate future threatens to disconfirm the nature of our present existence.[4] Dread is therefore the dread of possibility; it transfixes the person it takes possession of in an endless present that is itself the undesired contemplation of futurity. (From what presently unseeable shape that cannot even be imagined does the supernatural hand come? Does it mean to comfort or threaten? When will it move? If it moves, what will it do? What does its existence say about my existence; what change does it imply?) For Ishmael, there is no dramatic resolution to his encounter with the hand, just a diminishment of his original emotion into puzzlement and occasional retrospective wonder. His "awful fear," though throwing him forward in time as it obliterates his present into an eternity, itself has no future; indecisive fear without a tangible object could not have a future unless its true object were recognized. Just as it has no real object, the experienced object of dread is nothing: nonbeing itself, the abyss of sheer potentiality, eternity, death in a universalized form that is paradoxically all the more intensely experienced for its abstraction. It is our death made general yet immediately and personally felt as an imminent presence; as such, it is the present apprehension of eternity, our ultimate future. In dread, we face the naught that annihilates; and no less than this was faced by Ishmael when he was sent to bed supperless by the best and most conscientious of stepmothers, to face an emptiness made manifest as a presence. Much later, as an adult nearing the end of a voyage driving on to catastrophe, Ishmael will characterize Ahab's world as a "step-mother world," both "cruel" and "forbidding" (CXXXII); for Ishmael, the metaphor is not sentimental, because it grows out of his own most deeply felt experience.

All of which is not to say that the childhood waking-dream is a "trauma" which somehow causes the world and character of Ishmael; to say that would require a priori belief in some particular causal metaphysic of psychology. The most *Moby Dick* warrants along such lines is given by Ishmael's own use of the dream: to explain a present situation, in that waking up to find Queequeg's arm thrown around him resembles to Ishmael the past situation strongly enough so that the memory of that past spontaneously occurs to him as, in a roundabout way, illuminating by its parallelism. While Queequeg's arm arouses no "awful fear," which is at the heart of the childhood experience, the feelings evoked by his "pagan arm" are "very similar, in their strangeness" to those accompanying the "supernatural hand." The parallelism is to be found in the "strangeness." The feelings about the hand are, it is true, much more intense; and they are recounted in much greater detail and length than those of the experience supposedly to be illuminated. Evidently, the earlier feelings are intrinsically more interesting to Ishmael. Why? Although they can shed some light on the later experience, nothing can shed light on them; they and their cause are absolute in their strangeness. Perhaps the later event is merely a diminishment of the former for the most obvious reason: Queequeg's pagan arm, however tattooed, however

odd, is at least attached to a visible body, so that arm and body together become a rough kind of index to the self inhabiting them,
however paradoxical the self of a gentle cannibal may be; while the
supernatural hand as it is experienced grows out of nothing visible,
absolute strangeness, nothingness itself. In short, the earlier event
contains the essence of the later: if it is characteristic of the strange
to be only relatively explicable, it is characteristic of nothingness to
resist any explanation whatever. Nothingness: the void, absence, non-
meaning, nonform, noncoherence—this is what secretly underlies the
present experience of Queequeg's arm concealed beneath the present's
merely relative strangeness. The past event is stronger than the
present because it is Ishmael's nature to be fascinated by the *quintes-
sentially* strange.

This is, I realize, a circular account. I have not explained Ishmael's
nature by his psychically fateful dream. But the supernatural hand
which materializes out of a stepmother's rejection is not given in the
book as an anterior cause of Ishmael's self and world. Instead, it is a
coexistent part of them: the present has called forth the past only
in response to *itself;* the past that answers to the present thereby
reveals that present to be founded in the confrontation of nothingness. Such explanation as there is is that this is true not only of one
particular incident in Ishmael's present and re-presented life but of
his whole life. Just before the supernatural hand came to him, Ishmael was achingly bored; just before he met Queequeg, he had
nothing on shore that could interest him. Ishmael's childhood boredom is natural to children; it needs no more explanation than he
gives it. But the adult boredom as an integral part of his character
is not explicable except in terms of psychological schemata not
derivable from the book itself. In terms of the book it is not explicable; moreover, as if boredom were near its secret center, the book
tends to conceal its presence, which can be inferred only from the
positive phase of boredom's dialectic: we never *see* Ishmael bored,
we only see him as an enthusiastic seeker of the interesting. But because a desire to know the exotic *torments* him, so that the search for
the interesting governs his life, we can posit the existence of his

condition; for this intense drive toward knowing the strange could not characterize a man unthreatened by boredom: "With other men, perhaps, such things would not have been inducements; but as for me, I am tormented by an everlasting itch for things remote" (I)— to other men "the interesting" would be merely one of many life categories, not the one thing that drives them everlastingly on. Whatever their cause, it is from Ishmael's recurrent alternations between the emptiness of boredom and the exotic fullness of the strange that the pattern of his life follows.

Recurrently, through boredom he perceives meaninglessness in world and self. Recurrently, he seeks out the interestingly strange, even to the extremes of horror and dread, to replace his sense of constricted emptiness with a sense of plenitude. But because near the heart of the strange is a final inexplicability, an ultimate uncertainty, this strange cannot provide what is at last necessary for an enduring experience of plenitude: certainty of meaning, and its attendant complacency. As the remedy gradually exhausts itself, the cycle must begin again. The recurrent moods in which Ishmael's universe is constituted are boredom, dread, and pervasive despair, the protean modes of confrontation of nothingness.

Moods and World

Begun as an escape from the meaninglessness of boredom, the night journey with Ahab into the realm of the interesting soon becomes a voyage of dread: "I, Ishmael, was one of that crew; my shouts had gone up with the rest; my oath had been welded with theirs; and stronger I shouted, and more did I hammer and clinch my oath, because of the dread in my soul" (XLI). Dread is a "wild, mystical, sympathetical feeling" (XLI)—Kierkegaard calls it a "sympathetic antipathy and an antipathetic sympathy." In dread, attraction is barely concealed behind the nebulously frightening. And this indecisive ambivalence, in its broad spectrum of intensities, defines Ishmael's feeling for most of the things of his world; in fact, largely defines that world.

The sea, for example, is a realm of ferocity, estrangement, and dissolution as well as of interest and even beauty. Though it invites thought, it necessarily defeats it by its constant mutability and formlessness. Air is mysteriously animated Being, powerful but invisible. Fire is the contrariety of all the elements in their essence. Light is necessary for illumination, yet deceitful. Motion is necessary to avoid stagnation and boredom, but it is circular and seems futile. The vortex can be emblematic of internal composure, but it is also a means to death. Vertical movement can break out of circularity, but it involves the terrors of self-dissolution. Those who have broken out of circularity can speak of what they have experienced only in the riddling language of madness. The body conceals even as it reveals; it can be equal to the self or split from it. As for the self, it is near yet remote, whole but divided, stable but changing. Other people are strangers, defeating both reason and love as means of access to them; seen directly, as comic figures or animated nature, they remain distant; experienced in soliloquy, they are self-divided, full of emptiness, and few clear judgments can be made of them. The causal sequences of time are uncertain, dominated by different forces at different instants, or else always fated. There may be no significance *in* things. The abysses of eternity and death remain shadowed. The past is unknowable and the future mere death. Repetition is the only certainty, but the ultimate nature of repetition is dubious. Going to sea to find a renewed sense of life is an existential paradox.

Ahab's summary statement puts all this together: "The dead, blind wall butts all inquiring heads at last" (CXXV). To Ishmael, the constant inquirer, most of the spatial and temporal universe remains a mystery, despite his many theories. He sees man imprisoned in time by past nonexistence and future death: "Our souls are like those orphans whose unwedded mothers die in bearing them: the secret of our paternity lies in their grave, and we must there to learn it" (CXIV). His metaphysical inquiries founder. In his world, if one posits reasons or causes, like the gods, for the existence and nature of things, one is soon faced, like Ahab, with an infinite regress: behind the controlling gods of the fire are superior gods, dimly seen.

If Ishmael's world were like the globe in the Hindu diagram, supported by an elephant itself standing on four turtles, what the turtles
stand on would not be thinkable, for even the monumental facticity
of a being like the whale is "unsourced." Obliterated as a familiar,
meaningful totality, the world necessarily becomes alienated from
Ishmael, just as his descriptive recreation of it makes it alien to us:
it is never *our* world; despite his endless introductions, it remains
remote. For us as for Ishmael its remoteness takes on the pervasive
color of uncertainty. Like Stubb, Ishmael wonders "whether the
world is anchored anywhere," and concludes only "if she is, she
swings with an uncommon long cable, though" (CXXI). Indeed, in
Ishmael's world so many reasons for the existence of things that
would anchor existence in an order dissolve before honest common
sense that the world itself comes to seem accidental. Even the idea
of fatality, however terrible for some it must prove if true, seems at
times like a childish fantasy despairingly wished to guarantee that
everything is not sheer flux and chance; and it is important to note
that the opposition between chance and fatality ("what's to be, will
be; and then again, perhaps it won't be, after all," XIX, says the
prophet Elijah) is an opposition that is unresolved to the end, when
Ishmael *is,* but might as well not be: "It so chanced," he says in the
epilogue, explaining his survival and the book's existence; but he
immediately goes on to say that the "chance" was "ordained" by
"the Fates," making the ending as ambiguous on this point as any
earlier part of the book.

As the book progresses, Being increasingly becomes tinged with
nonbeing. In such a world, like Ishmael, we all *are,* but might as
well not be. For much of the book we hardly know *where* we are—
true places are not down on any map[5]—as the course of the novel
wanders from plot to anecdote to documentation, bogus and real,
to speculation and back to plot, which hovers over the digressions
like the memory of an eternal plan. Such a world remains mute to any
question of *why;* if it speaks at all, what it says to Ishmael as our
surrogate is *death.*

All of which is why the chapter (XLII) devoted to the analysis of whiteness, a chapter which progresses from the consideration of the color of one whale to the "great principle of light" operating secretly upon the entire "palsied universe," may profitably be set against Ishmael's general sense of things; for in analyzing the whiteness "that above all things appalled" him, he concentrates his essential response to his universe, and once more organizes and makes explicit the emotion in which that subjective universe is primarily founded.

The White World

Ishmael's reasoning on the subject of whiteness is characteristically dialectical and circular, because such mental motion is descriptively most appropriate to his ambiance.

His dialectical analysis begins with a statement of the most common associations of whiteness, a color that may call to mind beauty, aristocracy, joy, innocence, benignity, honor, justice, divinity, spotlessness—"whatever," in short, "is sweet, and honorable, and sublime"; yet, "there . . . lurks an elusive something in the innermost idea of this hue, which strikes . . . panic to the soul." Whiteness is polarized in this way because, when "coupled with any object terrible in itself," it heightens "that terror to the furthest bounds." For example, "the irresponsible ferociousness" of the white bear "stands invested in the fleece of celestial innocence and love; and hence, by bringing together two such opposite emotions in our minds," frightens us "with so unnatural a contrast." It is as if the contradictory emotions evoked by the dialectical movement within the mind cancel each other out, leaving nothing, and therefore dread. Yet to assert this makes whiteness only one half responsible for the dread, and this is clearly not so: self-canceling emotional opposition is insufficient to account for the terror of the white bear, for "were it not for the whiteness, you would not have that intensified terror." There must be something inherent in whiteness itself; and the fact that creatures not in themselves ferocious or terrible—an albatross, "the White Steed of the Praries," a human Albino—can evoke "spiritual wonderment and pale dread," "trembling reverence and awe," repellence and shock; this fact is evidence that the final source of emotional ambiguity is to be found in the color itself.

Nature herself assumes the power of whiteness to intensify dread when "in her least palpable but not the less malicious agencies" she enlists "among her forces this crowning attribute of the terrible": thus, "the gauntleted ghost of the Southern Seas" is called "the White Squall"; "human malice" chooses white as a "potent auxiliary" when "the desperate White Hoods of Ghent murder their bailiff in the market-place"; ghosts are white, death is white; it is because white is the color of "supernaturalism" that it "appals." There seems to be something no less than ontological about whiteness that loosens it from the contingent power of ordinary feelings: "in his other moods, symbolize whatever grand or glorious thing he will by whiteness, no man can deny that in its profoundest idealized significance it calls up a peculiar apparition to the soul."

That whiteness is ontological becomes the burden of the chapter's remaining argument. The essential status of the color is implied, first, by the effect it has on types of "unread" men of "untutored ideality"; second, by the same effect that the color "stripped of all direct associations" has on more sophisticated men who have no *reason* to be repelled by it, but nevertheless are. Neutralized whiteness neutrally observed can evoke "an eyeless statue in the soul," or overwhelm the spirit in a peculiar mood of "gigantic ghostliness" or "exert . . . a spectralness over the fancy." The sailor who notes his ship "sailing through a midnight sea of milky whiteness" feels "a silent, superstitious dread" not because of the proximity of dangerous reefs—his lead tells "him he is still off soundings"—but because of the "hideous whiteness" itself; the sailor who beholds "the scenery of the Antarctic seas . . . views what seems a boundless church-yard grinning upon him with its lean ice monuments and splintered crosses," and feels, again, "dread." The ruins of the city of Lima escape time: their white color, in not admitting "the cheerful greenness of complete decay," keeps the ruins "for ever new" and thereby reveals "a higher horror" to the eye. Whiteness, in these examples, is not merely "the prime agent in exaggerating the terror of objects otherwise terrible"; it is the one factor that consistently invests with terror "appearances whose awfulness . . . almost solely consists in [the fact of their being white, especially when this color is] exhibited under any form approaching to muteness or universality."

Aware that his argument, despite its imitation of logic, is dependent on a piling up of examples that involve emotion more than reason, Ishmael is once more constrained to say that he is not surrendering "to a hypo"; that whiteness escapes categories as well as ordinary moods; that he is accurately describing "its profoundest idealized essence." In desperation, his final gambit is to use the dread that underlies his response to this color as itself an argument, just as, in the New Bedford chapel facing the tombstones,[6] he used emotions to get at the facts of death: a "strong young colt" foaled and raised far from the region of buffalo will react with fear to a buffalo robe, and thereby display "the instinct of the knowledge of demonism in the world"; Ishmael asserts that his reaction to whiteness is like that of the colt to the alien hide. Like the colt, he cannot define what he fears, nor describe it rationally, yet he knows by the very strength of his reaction that "nameless things" worthy of his fear somewhere must exist; for, "though in many of its aspects this visible world seems formed in love, the invisible spheres were formed in fright." If the invisibilities of the world were formed "in fright"—whatever that formula may mean; and the grammatical possibilities are extensive—such fright so stated is abstracted from any specific cause in order to wander in a void. Ishmael's intention here is of a piece with his calling the fear that whiteness characteristically evokes "nameless horror" and "nameless terror"; for the fright linked with invisibility can also not be named, since it too has as yet no object. Its future is not yet here. Like the Vermont colt, Ishmael *knows* only because he fears; perhaps, to twist Descartes, at this point he *is* only because he fears.

With his last circular and emotional argument, Ishmael arrives once more at his very first point: that whiteness may connote virtue or evil: "it is at once the most meaning symbol of spiritual things, nay, the very veil of the Christian's Deity; and yet . . . it is . . . the intensifying agent in things the most appalling to mankind." This describes Ishmael's initially dialectic stance, the point of departure which he left in order to explore one half of the dialectic. None of his tentative explanations has satisfied him; no synthesis has emerged; the dialectic has existed only to come full circle. In his exploration he has overwhelmed us with examples, some of them so farfetched they clearly reflect the ponderings of a man trying to think the unthinkable by surrounding it. In short, rationally, Ishmael has not gotten very far: "But not yet have we solved the incantation of this whiteness, and learned why it appeals with such power to the soul." Emotionally, however, he has gotten considerably further: he has used his extreme examples to dramatize his own extremity. His argument, as well as whiteness, is "incantation." As a result, Ishmael may not be able to encapsule the concept of whiteness in a formula, but he has taught himself, and us, at least what whiteness *feels* like: he has summoned up its compulsive, ambiguous, desperate dread, and this, finally, gives him a certain power over its essence.

Which is why, after his concluding recapitulation of helplessness before the idea of whiteness, he is able to break through (largely by means of how whiteness feels) to the summary, and quite Olympian, perspective implied by his rhetorical questions: "Is it that by its indefiniteness it shadows forth the heartless voids and immensities of the universe, and thus stabs us from behind with the thought of annihilation, when beholding the white depths of the milky way?" Voids, immensities, annihilation from where it is least expected; whiteness is a negation, which is what is implied by the second question also: "Or is it, that as in essence whiteness is not so much a color as the visible absence of color, and at the same time the concrete of all colors; is it for these reasons that there is such a dumb blankness, full of meaning, in a wide landscape of snows—or a colorless all-color of atheism from which we shrink?" The dumb blankness is full of meaning: the meaning itself is the whiteness, the blankness, the emptiness. White is colorless, yet an all-color; its qualities thereby cancel out, leaving the blankness of nothing, which inspires our dread. It might also be noted that, however implicitly affirmative their answers might be, Ishmael's words putting forth these negations are questions, not answers. Questions create a waiting, an emptiness, a void to be filled by the future. Ishmael will not supply answers because the heart of his emotion-conveyed insight is absence, not presence.

As white is the color of the dreadful, it might also be called a boring color. Despite its containment of all tonal possibilities, it has itself no variety. Suggesting "muteness and universality," it escapes time; yet to make it speak to us, Ishmael has catalogued its manifestations at almost tedious length and duration, adducing the most varied creatures and events of earth, air, and water until there seems little possibility of escape from his elemental piling up of examples; until, that is, the frightening stellar prospect of immense voids and a cold landscape of snows suggest not a perceivable order but a perceivable chaos: darkness visible rather than light: atheism, not the presence of God. The preceding examples from the realms of earth, air, and water become in the end subsumed under "the great principle of light" itself, a light which then floods the universe, isolating in retrospect each elemental instance so that everything in existence is suddenly stripped of its false colors and revealed in its elementally boring whiteness; and with the whiteness of dread characterizing all animate and inanimate nature, "the palsied universe lies before us like a leper."[7]

Here, the emotion that constitutes white makes vibrantly visible as a presence the nothingness with which all existence is secretly sickened. Ishmael in this chapter has writ large the "supernatural hand" of his childhood; he has given it visibility and extension, if not form.

Moby Dick—the Focus of Despair

What gives it such form as it has is, as Ishmael says, "the Albino Whale."

Because Moby Dick—of "all these things . . . the symbol"—becomes "at times"[8] for Ishmael the summary instance of the nature of the white world, it is no more than fitting that this encyclopedic creature appears on stage only at the end, literally to provide the book's ultimate occasion for the confrontation of man and animate whiteness. As the Pequod sails "due eastward for the earliest sun" (CXXXIV)—that source of white light with which Moby Dick is here, as elsewhere,[9] linked—toward the "White Whale's own peculiar ground" (CXXVI) and the rendezvous there which will give only the dubious illumination of death, the pace of the book increases: the digressions become less discursive, the chapters pile up and get shorter,[10] the plot more openly controls the book. And as the book breathlessly nears its conclusion, the depth, nature, and significance of that conclusion are foreshadowed by a series of demonic reversals: an obscene archbishop presides over a black mass; Ahab's harpoon is forged out of twelve rods and baptized by the blood of three pagans; dark but precise prophecies augur the future; a "gale comes from the eastward, the very course Ahab is to run for Moby Dick" (CXIX) bringing with it corpusants that light up the ship's three masts with nine flames; birds, possibly emissaries from invisible sky gods, assault Ahab. The death that is part of the business of whaling is brought nearer and made both real and strange by Queequeg's ritual preparations for it; by "the first man of the Pequod" to mount "the mast to look out for the White Whale on the White Whale's own peculiar ground" (CXXVI) falling, to drown in the depths of Moby Dick's sea; by the disappearance of a boat during the Rachel's encounter with the object of the Pequod's quest; by the baptism of the Pequod with the spray from a sea burial while passing a ship "most miserably misnamed the Delight" (CXXXI). The surfaces of the water world become especially deceptive, as in "The Gilder"; above that surface, meanings and situations change without warning: chasing whales through the straits of Sunda, Ahab finds himself chased by pirates; the Pequod's compass is reversed during the electrical storm; another measuring device (the log and line) fails; Queequeg's coffin, "the very dreaded symbol of grim death, by a mere hap" becomes "the expressive sign of help and hope of most endangered life" (CXXVII).

Thus approached by a series of ritual inversions and reversals, when Moby Dick finally appears, his vaunted awfulness is expressed in words echoing those used to define "the silent stillness of death" (XLII) that characterizes the white shark (a "transcendent" horror which, like the polar bear, induces contradictory, self-canceling emotions in the observer): as the shark swims with a "white gliding ghostliness of repose," Moby Dick swims with "a gentle joyousness —a mighty mildness of repose in swiftness" (CXXXIII). Not just effortless motion, but motion coupled with rest: Moby Dick appears to us as an existence in process, yet static. His unity is dialectical. Because it is, his aspects are contradictory: his "quietude" is a mask for violence, "the vesture of tornados"; a "grand god" who can splendidly bridge antithetic matter as he "booms his entire bulk into the pure element of air" (CXXXIV), he is also "devilish" as he displays "malicious intelligence" dallying "with the doomed craft." As the sum of all whales, he unites the contrarieties of all whiteness: he is the white whale, not a white whale.

Musing on the mysteries of wind and weather, and nearing this elusive creature, Ahab has an insane insight on the third and final day of the chase:

> Here's food for thought, had Ahab time to think; but Ahab never thinks; he only feels, feels, feels; *that's* thinking enough for any man! to think's audacity. God only has that right and privilege. Thinking is, or ought to be, a coolness and a calmness; and our poor hearts throb, and our poor brains beat too much for that.   [CXXXV]

Like Ishmael, Ahab has *thought* a great deal. Unlike Ishmael, he has reached conclusions on which he is about to stake his life; but here, just before he gets his last chance to prove his thought, Ahab momentarily reaches a negative, Ishmaelean sense of mental possibility: only God can think. What men call thought is founded in feeling, and is not distinguishable from feeling, so that thought is separable neither from the thinker's consciousness nor yet from the thinker's situation and mood. Thought therefore has no objective measure, no ultimate empirical test to validify it in the world. Finally, it is only on his dread that Ishmael can stake his impassioned thought that there are real invisibilities in the dark world worthy of his fear; it is only on his pain that Ahab can passionately stake his thought that the gods are evil, and only his final pain will exist to confirm his reasoning. At the end of the book the creamy white vortex of water pulls toward itself all questions in the forms of the askers of them, overwhelming all except one with the arbitrariness of perfect mystery. The white whale answers no one in human language; its inevitable, predicted, ritual climactic appearance is followed by its silent, unnoted disappearance, leaving the great shroud of the *surface* of the sea to roll on in endless repetition. Fought and hunted for three fierce days, Moby Dick, to Ishmael the fortuitously—or fatedly —surviving "third man" (CXXXV), is the dread, indefinable, unlimited, illuminating truth of Salamander giants finally born (on the blazing equator: the mid-point: the balance of values foreshadowed by the whale's talisman doubloon) at the end of a night journey begun on Christmas day.

Articulating boredom, the prereflective perception of the absence of certain meaning, into dread, the prereflective confrontation of nonbeing, this new truth can inspire, chiefly despair. And just as questioner and question must mirror each other distortingly or accurately, the despair may take various human forms. It may be a madness, reflecting inner and outer void, as it is with Pip ("He's missing. Pip! Pip! Ding, dong, ding! Who's seen Pip?" CXXIX) who early saw God's foot upon the treadle of the loom in the form of "multitudinous, God-omnipresent, coral insects, that out of the firmament of waters heaved the colossal orbs" (XCIII); so that for Pip a final confrontation with the white whale is not necessary, and he remains below in Ahab's cabin "in the ship's full middle" (CXXIX). Ahab, facing the possibility of total absence of meaning in his secret, momentary doubts ("Sometimes I think there's naught beyond," XXXVI), despairingly wills to be defiant; in his defiant despair is his insane strength,[11] his defiance *of* despair. Hypocrisy before the whale's world is also despair; thus Starbuck, as the white whale is neared:

> "Tell me not of thy teeth-tiered sharks, and thy kidnapping cannibal ways. Let faith oust fact; let fancy oust memory; I look deep down and do believe."

And Stubb:

> "I am Stubb, and Stubb has his history; but here Stubb takes oaths that he has always been jolly!"   [CXIV]

For Ishmael, the white whale is not really a particular case, a special instance of meaning in the world, but a summary statement of all worldly meaning as animate whiteness. Yet, for Ishmael, the white whale summarizes all instances of whiteness only "at times" (see above, p. 119, note 8): even the certainty of indefinite nothingness is itself uncertain.[12] Which, for Ishmael, compounds the nothingness by raising it to a power of itself; and allows for the potential correctness even of Ahab's "reductive" allegorization of the white whale as "evil."[13]

The Nature and Forms of Despair

"Call me Ishmael," we are told. But that name is equivocally stated, despite the abruptly imperative form of its declaration. The narrator precisely does *not* say that his name *is* Ishmael; or even that he is called Ishmael as a kind of nickname. "Call me Ishmael," he says, and immediately the diction of affable informality followed by the shock of the biblical name which is both formal and highly unlikely puts us in the presence of someone who for reasons of his own would rather not say who he really is.

If "Ishmael" is self-adopted, it is, with all its allusiveness, doubtless a more accurate designation of him than its sayer's real name, for it clearly signifies his sense of himself and his world. But because behind the show of affability a real name is withheld, Ishmael remains to some extent a stranger, and a man in a false position; and because he does, as soon as the self-bestowed name is spoken, the shadow of nothingness is upon the book.

That shadow lengthens when we note the contradictory details that slips of memory betray the narrator into. The playful but ultimately serious hyperbole, intended to win us over; the authoritative reporting of unknowable or imaginary events; the fanciful lies, such as the Town-Ho's story—these darken the shadow. "Ishmael," we soon discover, is a storyteller in every sense; he tells us a fish story that, like most fish stories, is partly true and partly false.

Yet he is not especially anxious to conceal this from us. On the contrary, "storyteller" is the first and continuing guise in which he presents himself. At times he explicitly discusses the problems of a storyteller in creating atmosphere and plausibility (see above, pages 5–7). At other times he shows himself manipulating the truth:

> "Do tell, now," cried Bildad, "is this Philistine a regular member of Deacon Deuteronomy's meeting? I never saw him going there, and I pass it every Lord's day."
>
> "I don't know anything about Deacon Deuteronomy or his meeting," said I, "all I know is, that Queequeg here is a born member of the First Congregational Church. He is a deacon himself, Queequeg is."
>
> "Young man," said Bildad sternly, "thou art skylarking with me—explain thyself, thou young Hittite. What church dost thee mean? answer me."
>
> Finding myself thus hard pushed, I replied . . .   [XVIII]

Caught out in a lie, Ishmael eludes Bildad's wrath by enthusiastic embroidery of his story's loose ends.[14] In content and circumstances, the incident is typical of Ishmael's lies, the facts of which if based on actuality are already highly interpreted by self-interested exegesis. More important, however, is what this sort of incident—the Town-Ho's story, though a more disinterested, virtuoso lie, is similar in this respect—suggests about the audience of an Ishmaelean lie: Ishmael lies to those who invite his mockery. He lies to the earnest ones of the earth: the owners, aristocrats, and authorities; the stern, the righteous, or the self-satisfied; all who because of the pompous security they command are gullible. He lies, in short, to the Bildads who in being false comforters take false comfort. He lies because he strongly suspects either that their truths are lies also; or that they use their truths like lies, for their own ends.

Similarly, Ishmael lies to us: the comfortable readers of adventure stories like *Typee, Omoo,* and *Moby Dick* who kill our boredom by distorting what boredom means. We are all in false positions, his attitude seems to say; and it says this at the same time that it says that *his* false position, because it is consciously chosen in full awareness of the alternatives, is more responsible and therefore, perversely, truer than the received and unexamined false positions of others; and in this attitude we may understand a major basis of Ishmael's respect for Ahab, whose defiant despair creates a personal truth so passionately thought-out and passionately willed that often reality crucially seems to conform to it. Like Kierkegaard, Ishmael is despairingly left with the idea that for man, in many complicated ways, subjectivity is truth; or, rather, the only truth is in subjectivity.

One result of all this is that for the pragmatic reader the prevalence of Ishmaelean lies, once recognized, must permeate with nonbeing everything that Ishmael says. Because anything is potentially untrue, the single and final reality of the events of the Pequod's last voyage is to be found in Ishmael's not wholly trustworthy mind. For such a reader, *Moby Dick's* foundations in the actuality that Ishmael pretends to report are very shaky ones: he can never lose his awareness that he is reading a *novel,* not something solid like the history or biography that Captain Veres prefer; moreover, he is reading a peculiarly self-subverting novel that pretends to be true (but clearly isn't) autobiography, which in turn disconcertingly combines features of epic, romance, and Menippean satire. Nowhere is there dry land. Nothing can be trusted to be what it seems, and the reader, if only for self-preservation, must have "doubts of all things earthly" (LXXXV). In a curious way, the reader is forced even against his will to share Ishmaelean attitudes.

But the situation is perhaps not so desperate. Consider the case of
Bulkington, the account of whom provides a reassuring example of
Ishmael's manipulation for his own purposes of reality. Bulkington
is the man "who in mid-winter just landed from a four years' dangerous voyage . . . unrestingly" pushes "off again for still another
tempestuous term" (XXIII) as the helmsman of the outsetting
Pequod. "A huge favorite" (III) with his previous shipmates aboard
the Grampus, Bulkington is a natural leader of men, and a man of
singular physique and mentality.

Yet after his appearance as the Pequod's helmsman in the "six-inch
chapter" called "The Lee Shore," he inexplicably disappears: "So far
as this narrative is concerned," Ishmael says of him, he will be "but
a sleeping-partner" (III). Given Bulkington's initial presentation,
his noble integrity and intelligence, he ought to have had, like Chek-
hov's pistol, a major function in the drama: leading the men against
Ahab, or, if convinced that Ahab is right, becoming a source of
strength for his captain. Yet Bulkington, who ought to be as weighty
as his name and body, disappears. Perhaps he died early in the voyage,
so that he was absurdly unable to assume the role implied for him;
but even this is not recorded. Why not?

The formal answer seems to lie in what *is* given of Bulkington's
role: he is the helmsman at the outset of the voyage, and thereafter
a "sleeping-partner." A helmsman directs the ship; a sleeping-partner
is commonly a partner whose existence is kept secret from the general
public, and who takes no overt part in the enterprise with which he
is involved even though his capital may dominate it.[15] Ishmael admits (or makes it up out of nothing) Bulkington's existence to us
but thereafter suppresses his presence, which finally exists as a "deep"
memory embodied in the "six-inch chapter" which is his "stoneless
grave" (XXIII). Because that memory is an explanation of Bulkington's motivation (see page 77, above), his motivation is what,
for purposes of the narrative, Bulkington becomes; as sleeping-
partner, that is what he *is*. The motivation attributed to him is a kind
of eternal drive toward knowing the truth: up until his last voyage
always voyaging, on this last voyage Bulkington faced conclusively

his own "ocean-perishing," and facing this final human reality has, according to Ishmael, allowed Bulkington to see "glimpses . . . of that mortally intolerable truth; that all deep, earnest thinking is but the intrepid effort of the soul to keep the open independence of her sea; while the wildest winds of heaven and earth conspire to cast her on the treacherous, slavish shore." Because his motivation here resembles that of both Ishmael and Ahab, comprehending the latter's will to absolute, ultimate knowledge as well as the former's compulsive mental integrity that must admit all contradictory speculation; and because this motivation is what Bulkington *is;* and because his Being-in-this-mode is the helmsman of the outsetting Pequod, thereafter becoming a sleeping-partner whose secret capital is part of the Pequod's value, Bulkington's literary existence is as a kind of animating and directive principle of the voyage. His being expresses that "the highest truth" resides only in the condition of "landlessness"—which is to say that it either (as Ahab thinks) may be found within landlessness, or (as Ishmael suspects) may be landlessness itself. Like Ishmael, Bulkington finds no final answers, but experiences the spirit in which the questions must be framed; like Ahab, he dies and becomes a grim "demigod," whose "apotheosis" is the chapter, as Ahab's is the book.

Bulkington is *used* by Ishmael allegorically. In this use he finds the role wherein, as far as the narrative is concerned, lies his chief reality. If Bulkington's literary existence is given us for the sake of what it means to Ishmael, and if that meaning "is" his spiritual presence, then his *actual* presence must be suppressed; for any one of his three probable roles in actuality would have conflicted with his Ishmael-conferred meaning: if Bulkington supported Ahab, he became the partisan of a delimited portion of the principle he reflects; if he fought Ahab, he similarly denied validity to what by virtue of Ishmael's initial presentation of him is part of himself, as well as competing with the white whale for the office of Ahab's antagonist (Bulkington would have been a more effectual human antagonist than Starbuck; but in Ishmael's intention only Moby Dick could be worthy of meeting Ahab conclusively); and, last, if Bulkington absurdly died before his natural leadership could play out its role, the direction and principle of the voyage would be too contrarily and specifically obliterated. For all such reasons, it does not matter that about Bulkington, Ishmael lies.

Ishmael's handling of Bulkington suggests, in fact, that we are not in danger of losing our bearings on his manipulated version of the Pequod's voyage because his major manipulations of reality— his hyperbole, irony, and lies—are in each case open to teleological analysis and, over all, are performed in the service of his vision of the meaning of the truth. In short, Ishmael is simply a writer of fiction. As such, his truth is born of his lies; and given the nature of his truth, it could exist only by virtue of them.

Ishmaelean truth, as Ishmael's total vision of the world manifests it, is the truth of relativity: "There is no quality in this world that is not what it is merely by contrast," he says early in the book (XI); "nothing exists in itself." If things exist only in relation to other things, and assume their qualities by virtue of contrast with other qualities, then just as truth must exist by virtue of lies, Being by virtue of nonbeing, so the self must exist by virtue of the not-self: "O Nature, and O soul of man!" says Ahab, "how far beyond all utterance are your linked analogies! not the smallest atom stirs or lives on matter, but has its cunning duplicate in mind."

Such an ontology must assume an epistemology in which mind and matter are similarly interdependent. The reality of life, Ishmael tells us in the very first chapter of his book, is physically "ungraspable." It exists as an "image" of a "phantom" of itself seen by the water-dreaming Narcissus (who is "all of us") in the shifting water-world, which, before it is depths, is reflecting surfaces. Life as man knows it is a phantom image that is experienced superficially and elusively in a momentary present; it is dependent on an unsuspected source which both projects and ambiguously (in the end, mistakenly) perceives it, a relation which prevents it from being directly confronted. The future's attempt to grasp the phantom's solidity must destroy the reality as well as its image. Reality, in other words, is so evasive because at the same time that the seen does not exist apart from the seer, it is nevertheless different from him; and because both terms exist only in tenuous relationship, consciousness cannot be escaped in order to grasp any objective presence. To mistake this, like Narcissus and Ahab, is to risk death.

Meaning, in such a relationship, is as inescapable as it is elusive; and, whatever else it may be, it is first of all *human* meaning, conferred by man in the process of living. Meaning is inescapable because it is generated in the act of perception itself; the very clarity of outline of an object belongs to the meaning that is present in the object's perception.[16] Meaning is human meaning because it existentially "is" only as the doubloon's value "is": conferred by man. Indeed, the doubloon chapter's chief function is to slow down the normal act of perception for the reader's edification: confronting the doubloon, each onlooker notices some details but not others, sees analytically or synthetically, perceives obverse or reverse, notes contexts or not, and in so doing creates partial and finite static value out of what must remain eternally itself and mute—a static value out of a coin which, nailed to the midpoint, is an integral part (the "navel," says Pip) of a ship that moves on a sea that moves on a world itself whirling through the shifting skies. If Ishmaelean man must confer meaning on *things,* the things are processional and the meaning is dictated by the changeable limits of his self-structured experience and the evanescent dominance of his moods. Meaning is an integral part of reality, but reality does not exist apart from consciousness. Reality and meaning *are* the relation of man and world; they are the quality of his concern with the things of his world: a coffin may "be" a coffin, but "by a mere hap" of man's purposeful concern it may also be a sea-chest, then a life buoy—ultimately, in its potentiality it "is" all three at once, for Ishmaelean Being is becoming and is therefore always touched with possibility; with, that is, nothingness.

On such assumptions is founded the assertion that the highest truth is to be found in landlessness alone; that it is "shoreless, indefinite as God" (XXIII). It is why at sea each gam suggests a potential, *established* view of the whale, even unto the status of national attitudes; because, in the end as in the beginning, the overwhelming, unarguable facticity of the whale can be elucidated *only* in terms "of what has been promiscuously said, thought, fancied, and sung of Leviathan, by many nations and generations, including our own" (from the "Extracts" supplied by a sub-sub-librarian).

It is the reason, also, that Ishmael himself resembles the mutability and shiftiness he experiences as his world; because there is nothing on which he can solidly base his existence in a universe of infinite possibility that at the same time is infinite repetition, a world both fated and free and therefore dreadful, Ishmael can only be these contrarieties, a modern Narcissus. Thus we are never told Ishmael's real name: to name is implicitly to define, but because he can see nothing certain he can will nothing with his total being; therefore, for us as for himself, he can *be* nothing definite. Unlike Ahab, he has no aspirations to sainthood.

As character, Ishmael is a sailor; as narrator, a storyteller. The sort of book this uncommon sailor writes follows from the self-world relation which is his reality. It is a book not surprisingly grounded, often, in despair, an emotion whose forms are as protean and dialectical as those of boredom and dread.

Theologically, despair is the despair of God's power to save one's soul. In doubting that power, God as God is doubted, as is the nature of ultimate truth. Certainly, Ishmael has many moments when his despair is overt and resembles the theological, as in the passage in which he experiences death as absolute disappearance (see above, page 16), or in his rejection of Christian hope in chapter XCVI: "All is vanity. ALL. This wilful world hath not got hold of unchristian Solomon's wisdom yet." However, Ishmael's theological doubts do not express themselves always in such melancholy tones. Quite evidently well-acquainted with the Bible, Ishmael admits to being a former believer ("I was a good Christian; born and bred in the bosom of the infallible Presbyterian Church," X) just before he humorously turns idolator with Queequeg. He cherishes "the greatest respect towards everybody's religious obligations, never mind how comical" (XVII). "Hell," he says cheerfully, "is an idea first born on an undigested apple-dumpling; and since then perpetuated through the hereditary dyspepsias nurtured by Ramadans" (XVII). No longer having doctrinal beliefs, he must needs be tolerant: "Heaven have mercy on us all—Presbyterians and Pagans alike—for we are all somehow dreadfully cracked about the head, and sadly need mending" (XVII). Without doctrine, he is, as he himself admits, a kind of pagan, "a savage, owning no allegiance but to the King of the Cannibals; and ready at any moment to rebel against him" (LVII). Beyond that, he is uncommitted, *even to paganism:* "Doubts of all things earthly, and intuitions of some things heavenly; this combination makes neither believer nor infidel, but makes a man who regards them both with an equal eye" (LXXXV); neither believer nor infidel, because no mere label will do.

Ishmael's minimal beliefs make him perhaps more prone to superficial mood swings than more solidly grounded citizens. Like "all sailors of all sorts" he is "more or less capricious," even "unreliable" (XLVI); he has lived in "the outer weather" and inhaled its "fickleness." Yet this very fickleness is a sign of the persistence of the despair that underlies it, a despair which is to be measured not only in specifically negative theological moments, but in the extent to which defeated hope pervades Ishmael's book.

The poet, says Emerson, meaning the term more broadly than versifier, is the sayer, the namer. Ishmael is a poet who names what he knows to be dreadfully nameless: he tells us of Timor Tom, New Zealand Jack, Don Miguel, and Moby Dick—all of them "famous whales" (XLV); but, if the final presence of Moby Dick may serve as index, the homeliness of these names falls absurdly short of defining the exotic wonder of their bearers' presences. What he does with individual whales, Ishmael does with the class of whales: a man who repeatedly protests his disbelief in the adequacy of systems, with humorous despair he offers us a "book" system of whale classification punningly based on the whale's most obvious feature—its sheer volume; a system in which his absurd and arbitrary ("Be it known that, waiving all argument, I take the good old fashioned ground that the whale is a fish," XXXII) terms must do "nothing less" than essay "the classification of the constituents of a chaos." Wishing to anatomize the idea of whaleness, he does so, literally, piece by piece, with actual whales; yet what his vision records is so contradictory he is repeatedly forced to confess that he can find no rational explanation to make everything cohere. Emotions as well as reason falter before the whale, as Ishmael shows us the creature in every light so that our fear, awe, wonder, sympathetic concern (in, for example, the episode involving baby whales in "The Grand Armada"), even our pity (for the frightened old bull whose sore Flask pricks) are aroused, and though each emotion will do for a time, no feeling is in itself sufficient to comprehend both the temporal and spatial magnitude of the phenomenon, as well as its occasionally intimate appearances. To go whaling is to go mentally adventuring among the exotic wonders of the water-world, but there is emptiness in the experience; and even at the beginning of his book, the narrator's despair intrudes each time he records his hopeful exhilaration anticipatory of adventure, yet systematically subverts it with foreshadowings of separation and death ("From that hour I clove to Queequeg like a barnacle; yea, till poor Queequeg took his last long dive," XIII) so that underlying the exuberance and ferocity of the pursuit is a constantly deepening sense of futility. Such despair proceeds from the narrator's knowledge of the voyage's end, but it has become pervasive because of his deeper consciousness of endings.

Each increase in consciousness, says Kierkegaard, involves increased despair; yet the possibility of despair is man's advantage over animals.[17] Ishmael says he is a savage; being a savage implies, as with Queequeg, "unconsciousness" (XIII), a being able to be always equal to oneself. The civilized man because of his wider conceptual awarenesses can be of several minds, therefore not equal to himself; and to the extent that this describes Ishmael, Ishmael is not a savage. His savagery is "true" only in certain aspects and those only intermittently or qualifiedly. With him, as with Ahab or the whale, again no simple formula will do.

Ishmael shares, for example, the patience of savages:

> Now, one of the peculiar characteristics of the savage in his domestic hours, is his wonderful patience of industry. An ancient Hawaiian war-club or spear-paddle, in its full multiplicity and elaboration of carving, is as great a trophy of human perseverance as a Latin lexicon. . . .
>
> As with the Hawaiian savage, so with the white sailor-savage. With the same marvelous patience, and with the same single shark's tooth, of his one poor jack-knife, he will carve you a bit of bone sculpture, not quite as workmanlike, but as close packed in its maziness of design, as the Greek savage, Achilles's shield; and full of barbaric spirit and suggestiveness . . .   [LVII]

Such artist-savages make material worthless in itself into things of value as, patiently, they literally fill their time with meaning. In telling his story, of course, so does Ishmael; with the difference that unlike the unreflective savages he describes he is conscious not only of what he is doing but of the contexts in which he is doing it. He is conscious, too, that the chief meaning with which he fills up time is built of uncertainty, contradiction, and irony, barbarically spirited and suggestive without doubt, but hardly clear in detail. The precision of savage art is not attainable for Ishmael because his mind must comprehend more things, all of which he "tries," achieving what he can (LXXIX): a kind of "careful disorderliness" (LXXXII). Even the attempt to be a *primitive* artist is futile, because although he has the patience he does not have the unconsciousness.

Despair shows some of its dialectical capacity in its grounding of Ishmaelean humor, the major purpose of which is to articulate discrepancies between the actual and the ideal. Repeatedly, the point of Ishmael's humor is a demonstration of the incomprehensibly angular absurdities of himself or others projected against the implicit possibilities of human grace, thereby drawing attention to missed connections in the universe. Early in the book Ishmael had said:

> a good laugh is a mighty good thing, and rather too scarce a good thing; more's the pity. So, if any one man, in his own proper person, afford stuff for a good joke to anybody, let him not be backward, but let him cheerfully allow himself to spend and be spent in that way. And the man that has anything bountifully laughable about him, be sure there is more in that man than you perhaps think for.   [v]

Later in the book Ishmael says: "that mortal man who hath more of joy than sorrow in him, that mortal man cannot be true—not true, or undeveloped. . . . The truest of all men was the Man of Sorrows" (XCVI). If despair is understood as the real ground of Ishmaelean humor, then the apparent contradiction between these two statements disappears:[18] like Stubb, the consistent humorist "has his history" (CXIV), and that history is not entirely a happy one. The humorist is what he is in relation to what he knows of sorrow. And that Ishmael is aware of despair as the potential basis for his own humor, his description of humorous despair shows:

> There are certain queer times and occasions in this strange mixed affair we call life when a man takes this whole universe for a vast practical joke, though the wit thereof he but dimly discerns, and more than suspects that the joke is at nobody's expense but his own. However, nothing dispirits, and nothing seems worthwhile disputing. He bolts down all events, all creeds, and beliefs, and persuasions, all hard things visible and invisible, never mind how knobby. . . . And as for small difficulties and worryings, prospects of sudden disaster, peril of life and limb; all these, and death itself, seem to him only sly, good-natured hits, and jolly punches in the side bestowed by the unseen and unaccountable old joker. . . . There is nothing like the perils of whaling to breed this free and easy sort of genial, *desperado* [italics added] philosophy . . .   [XLIX]

If the universe in this hyena mood seems like an obscure practical joke, the literary world Ishmael creates for us is often mined with hidden banter. Often this is obscene. Sometimes it lurks as potential meaning where it has no business to be: "Of erections, how few are domed like St. Peters!" (LXVIII). Another instance seems to be when Pip, after equating the doubloon with the ship's "navel," which all the lookers-at are "on fire to unscrew" (XCIX), asks portentously: "But, unscrew your navel, and what's the consequence?"—a question which only too readily brings to mind the punch line of the old joke about the Hindu mystic.[19] Sometimes the nonpertinence of the potential ribaldry can be staggering. Lawrance Thompson, for example, holds that the chapter "A Squeeze of the Hand," so important to critics who see the book's social-ethical admonitions as final, is secretly obscene.[20] Insisting upon a nonwhaling meaning for the word "sperm," he naturally finds the whole passage full of the sort of "accumulated off color word play" that, if indeed there, is positively Shakespearean in its strained bawdiness (even "country" makes its appearance):

> Would that I could keep squeezing that sperm for ever! For now, since by many prolonged, repeated experiences, I have perceived that in all cases man must eventually lower, or at least shift, his conceit of attainable felicity; not placing it anywhere in the intellect or the fancy; but in the wife, the heart, the bed, the table, the saddle, the fire-side, the country; now that I have perceived all this, I am ready to squeeze case eternally. In thoughts of the visions of the night, I saw long rows of angels in paradise, each with his hands in a jar of spermaceti.

In this passage, and throughout the four paragraphs preceding it, Thompson finds Ishmael-Melville ridiculing by his obscenity the idea of Christian brotherhood. While there is no doubt that Ishmael-Melville is capable of this sort of word play—"archbishoprick" (XCV), about which there can be no question, proves it—nevertheless, the hypothesized bawdry of "A Squeeze of the Hand" is so *very* strained, in addition to being violently out of congruence with the

lyrical rhetoric of at least the crucial paragraph just quoted (the self-
conscious sentimentality of the preceding paragraphs makes them
more plausible game), that the hidden presence of obscenity here
seems less certain than Thompson says it is. The real difficulty is that
all such obscenity must finally be in the eye of the beholder, for the
passage itself contains merely the grammatical possibility of obscenity. Yet it does contain that (and so do passages throughout the
book); and because it does, once the sincerity of the expressed sentiments is doubted, the words themselves can make us uncomfortable
without ever *necessarily* resolving themselves into either democratic
pietism or scurrilous anti-Christianity.

Perhaps, in short, precisely that irresolution is one literary function of such passages. In the chapter in question, the democratic
sentiments are undermined by the overt terms in which they are
presented: it is explicitly "a strange sort of insanity" that comes over
Ishmael to lead him to his "loving feeling," which is then dealt with
in hyperbole appropriate to "insanity"; while the ideals of landed
comfort are covertly undermined by Ishmael's continued bachelor-
voyaging, for he has failed to choose the self and life he urges us to
choose; and both *may* be further subverted by covert obscenity. What
we have in such passages is a kind of willful destruction of specific
meaning, meaning that is potential at several levels, but on no level
is finally asserted.[21]

Here humor has shaded into the problematics of Ishmaelean irony,
wherein no firm standpoint is offered the reader, and his wishes tend
to be projected into the material to provide one, the reader thereby
being forced to become part of what he reads. Such irony reflects—
just as the implicit rationale of lying does—the attitude of a man
who knows he does not know. It is the attitude of negative intellectual freedom that allows all standpoints to be playfully adopted
for the moment. Committed to nothing, the Ishmaelean ironist can
mockingly play with everything, as a result of which everything he
touches is eerily tinged with the color of mere possibility: his ironies,
like his lies, are "white."

Because they are, they become part of the methods by which Ishmael constructs a literary universe in which many meanings cannot be certified, a universe that reflects his own experienced universe and makes the Ishmaelean self a type of the alienated mind of fluid contrarieties. Here, conventional theological despair that doubts God shows its links with Kierkegaardian despair which with every increase of consciousness is increasingly uncertain that there is such a thing as a true self; for with no positive beliefs to characterize him, Ishmael can hardly be a continuously unified character. And, as has been suggested, others in Ishmael's book parallel his mode of despair: Pip's despair reflects inner and outer void, Ahab's becomes an intensity of selfhood that conceals a blank, Stubb's jolly despair hides his history (presumably one involving infidelities by his "juicy little pear" of a wife who gives parties to the "last arrived harpooneers" while he is away, XXXIX),[22] Starbuck despairingly wills to be the self of his old land faith despite the kidnapping cannibal ways of the sea that would deny the fundamental bases of that self. In each instance, the Being of personal identity is related to inner and outer nonbeing, existing in intimate conjunction with it.

Indeed, when Ishmael survives at the end supported by an empty coffin, a thing significant of death has come to signify life by virtue of accident working together with man's forming intentions, and the survival can be read as in part a reflection of the book's ontology wherein Being is radically dependent on nonbeing. Taking this one step further, one might say that Ishmael survives also by virtue of the book itself recording his survival; he survives therefore as an artist, and as a rather desperado artist whose desperation reaches into his book's style. It is, as Constance Rourke noted, an oral style. As such it is a highly personal style that creates its own implicit dramatic situation which suggests, at first, that Ishmael has cornered one auditor in, say, a bar, and spins him a yarn full of arguments and asides of what happened one memorable voyage. As the book progresses, the implied situation of narrator and auditor quickly shifts to that of a practiced storyteller now writing a sometimes awkward book for anyone at all to read, but an anyone addressed personally from time to time to recall something of the original storytelling situation. Ishmael therefore remains an habitual raconteur convivially telling tales, like the Town-Ho's, in bars, like Lima's Golden Inn; and because his tale of a whale is obsessively told—the product of almost total recall, invention, and what can best be termed extensive scholarly research—it may be suggested that the narrator is *driven* to tell it, as if he were a younger version of the ancient mariner, and his book the end result of many compulsive rehearsals. Ishmael is compelled to report and create meaning in what happened to him both despite, and because of, his sense of the uncertainty of meanings available to temporal man. Once more, Kierkegaard's categories can help to place the situation: if Ahab's response to despair is in its special way religious, and Starbuck's finally ethical, Ishmael's, beginning with his tormenting drive to seek out "the interesting," is aesthetic.

And that Ishmael's response is aesthetic to the point of his writing a book is sufficient explanation for his survival. He does not survive because of some merit on his part; to argue this—that what Ishmael has learned is what allows him to be saved, that Ishmael lives right or sees things in reasonable perspective while Ahab does not—to argue this is to assume an ethical universe of some sort: a tragically lopsided one in which innocents, like Pip, and good men, like Starbuck, die horribly precisely because of Ahab's moral-perceptional errors even though Ishmael does not. But whether the universe has any ethical character at all, lopsidedly tragic or otherwise, is a major part of what is in question in the first place; the argument assumes what it must demonstrate. Ishmael's book is in this respect prior to tragedy, though Ahab's story may well not be. His survival is therefore prior to all ethics, and the existentially sufficient reason for his survival is that what transcends death in time is art: art is what in fact does survive, often accidentally, and about its survival and Ishmael's as artist storyteller there is very little ethical that can, it seems to me, be convincingly posited.

Insofar as Ishmael's book exists in order to record his manner of survival, it exists in order to exist its writer as a dialectical being. Negatively, the narrator becomes so involved with the not-self that he is often in danger of losing himself as a character in it—in events and in others, as if by virtue of his negative capability he experiences fully his own nonbeing as an analogue to the universal void. Positively, the narrator becomes most a "character" through his humor, which points out and reflects inner and outer limitations, but which also tends at times toward an optimism that can experience the naughting ambiguity of self and universe as the plenitude of intellectual freedom: as a nearly infinite number of things in the world and a multitude of potential meanings arising out of the interrelation of these things with men's minds which gives Ishmaelean man the real freedom to worship no unworthy gods, but instead to try all things, to explore, and by exploring to create his own world of meanings. One might summarize the self of the Ishmaelean narrator as that of an artist who has constructed, as Melville's contemporary Flaubert hoped to,[23] a highly personal, stylized work: a something founded on nothing in the face of a nothing, a something which creates Ishmael's own ambivalent self for him and for us, and gives its peculiarly problematic existence to his world.

7. Conclusion: The Ishmaelean Creation of Meaning

Ishmael insists that his final whale must not be understood as a "hideous and intolerable allegory" (XLV) in the course of arguing that Moby Dick is first of all an actual whale. He does not mean by this that his whale has no meaning beyond itself, for he himself tries to get at such a meaning in his chapter on its whiteness, which deals with what the creature "was" to *him*.

Yet, as Northrop Frye has noted in *Anatomy of Criticism*, "all commentary is allegorical interpretation, an attaching of ideas to the structure of poetic imagery" (p. 89). Considering the strong thematic interest of the kind of book Ishmael has produced, he would seem to be requiring an impossibility of the practical critic. Certainly, in matters other than the whale, the injunction does not hold for himself, since Ishmael does in fact write explicit allegory in such chapters as "Fast-Fish and Loose-Fish" and "The Monkey-rope," and Bulkington is clearly an allegorical figure.

When he does so, though, it should be noted that Ishmael's explicit allegory is discontinuous. It is a matter of chapters rather than an unbroken sequence of systematic meaning throughout the book. Even his strongly *implicit* allegory is not serially coherent: the Pequod, for example, may carry aboard it all the races of mankind, and thus tentatively suggest an allegorical world-ship "on its passage out" (VIII),[1] but as soon as it meets another ship also containing men, that reference is submerged. The allegory here exists only long enough to assert the hidden typicality of this seemingly untypical ship, then its presence fades.

Perhaps the whale is discontinuously allegorical, too. But Ishmael's allegory elsewhere is either explicit, containing its own interpretive commentary, or heavily implicit. The whale is not handled that way. Further, Ishmael's insistence on the whale's actuality is vehement. Nevertheless, the whale has meaning, meaning which is somehow not allegorical.

In the contradiction, Ishmael would seem to be making the usual nineteenth-century English and German distinction between allegory and symbol, most familiar to us, perhaps, in Coleridge:

> Now an allegory is but a translation of abstract notions into a picture-language which is in itself nothing but an abstraction from objects of the senses. . . . On the other hand a symbol . . . is characterized by a translucence of the special in the individual, or of the general in the special, or of the universal in the general, above all, by the translucence of the eternal through and in the temporal. It always partakes of the reality which renders it intelligible; and while it enunciates the whole, abides itself as a living part in that unity of which it is the representative.
>
> [*The Statesman's Manual*, Appendix B][2]

Allegory, in other words, is mere technique. It involves the substitution of images for ideas, the latter usually being conceived first. Symbolism begins with the object, probably first experienced in existence, then embodied in the literary work: an object which somehow reveals a reality that metaphysically goes beyond sensory perception. In short, the symbolist does not just make use of a mechanical technique, he "sees" rather hazily something that he thinks is mysteriously contained within the symbolic object, something which is perhaps beyond his analytic powers of conception.

As Newton Arvin has observed, even though there was no real distinction in mid-nineteenth-century American literary usage between the words "symbol" and "allegory," nevertheless "America was already symbolist in everything but the program."[3] Here, in some dim way Ishmael seems to be making the kind of distinction so usual today; but, in the context of his subjective literary universe, he seems to be saying something that goes further than the insistence that his whale is actual before it has meaning. This is implied in what must seem to him to be "hideous and intolerable" about allegory, and it tends to reverse part of the usual nineteenth-century distinction.

If, in Ishmael's world, meaning is constantly generated in the dynamic relation between man's consciousness and his world, the use of allegory would violate this sense of meaning. Because allegory is a rhetorical method employing more or less systematically preconceived static conceptual reference, to allegorize the white whale would be to deform the category of something that actually exists for Ishmael as successive aspects: to deform it in the very act of giving it the static certainty of a form. What would be "hideous" would be the formal deformation. What would be "intolerable" would be the violation of the "plain facts" (XLV) of existential truth in its processional temporality, for it would be to see the white whale as existing *only* in Platonic eternity and not in time, when the latter is a given fact and the former merely possible.

Allegory, of course, can be written on purely secular matters, because it is a technique of manipulating ideas which themselves may refer to any level of reference. Historically, however, explicit allegory such as Dante's or Spenser's had tended to be written in the service first of all of religious, metaphysical views of the nature of being that were highly doctrinal. Its use had generally implied that the writer was aware of a static reality more real than the merely existential, and its images therefore tend to become less real than the eternal ideas they represent, ideas which ought therefore to claim greater interest than their vehicles. (In practice, in good allegory, of course, this is never true.)[4]

Ishmael's objection to allegory lies partly in his assumption that normal, ethical man is simply not privy to the conditions of religious eternities. The images of actuality must be such a man's initial interest; the temporal truths of ethical humanity must therefore seek their own literary method. (Because religious man may just possibly have access to the conditions of eternity, Ahab may or may not escape the implications of the injunction; but Ishmael clearly does not.) The fact that when not dealing with the white whale Ishmael sometimes allegorizes must be taken to be a partial inconsistency. It is quite consistent with allegory's ability to handle secular matters, but it tends toward violation of Ishmael's sense of processional meaning, as if here his Ahabian urge toward certainty has broken the integrity of his experience of uncertainty, so that the resulting lie becomes another sign of his despair: the inconsistency easily fits his world of despair. Yet even here there is at least minimal fidelity to a processional standard of the humanly available truth, for Ishmael allegorizes only discontinuously: time interrupts his Ideas.

That in the matter of the ultimate whale Ishmael does not allegorize seems probable if only because there is so very little critical agreement on what a satisfactory allegorical reference for Moby Dick might be.[5] Indeed, I suspect that many readers of Ishmael's book resent attempts to pin a label on the whale, as if this whale had in itself some power to escape the Heisenberg Indeterminacy Principle (to know something is to change it) of literature by resisting with more than ordinary force the tendency of rational commentary to convert the nature of symbol into allegory by the demonstration of a link between image and prematurely limited idea, a linkage which then comes to seem a necessary one to the convinced or converted reader. But this whale remains itself because no globally satisfactory conceptual designation for it has been advanced; if Ishmael's recreation of the whale is faithful to his implicit literary precept, no such conception *can* be advanced, because the whale exists first of all in time.

If temporal truth must seek its own literary method, that method in Ishmael's case, so most critics agree, turns out to be symbolism, the use of which, much more innately than the historical use of allegory, implies a metaphysical view of the nature of being; but, most typically, a nondoctrinal one. Since symbolism is all things to all men, it shall be my concern in what follows to describe briefly that symbolism which is specifically Ishmaelean, as it seems to operate in the white whale against the context of Ishmael's subjective literary universe.

Northrop Frye (page 92) calls the white whale an "heraldic symbol": "a central emblematic image" which "combines the qualities of Carlyle's intrinsic symbol with significance in itself, and the extrinsic symbol which points quizzically to something else." Further, such an emblematic image is "closely related to if not identical with" that "kind of image described by Mr. Eliot as an objective correlative," the latter being defined as an "image that sets up an inward focus of emotion . . . and at the same time substitutes itself for an idea."

The doubleness of reference Frye attributes to the heraldic symbol seems to me a useful place to begin. The whale is significant in itself, yet points quizzically to something else. It remains numinous and mute.

It remains mute, first, because Ishmael cannot rationally comprehend it. Before its final disappearance it behaves too astoundingly; its motives remain persistently obscure;[6] its final presence is so much vaster than human imagination can conceive a mere animal to be; it is unreasonably, exceptionally *white* when "blackness is the rule among almost all whales" (XXXII). It is, in short, so full of contrariety that it is not manageable under the aspect of causality; of all whales, it is most "unsourced," least explicable. Therefore it cannot be structured categorially, and whatever idea it points toward is quizzical indeed.

The whale remains mute, second, because Ishmael cannot even perceptually comprehend it. It cannot be structured sensationally because, like all whales, it has no face (LXXXVI). It does have features—a jaw, teeth, a solid white buttress of a forehead, scars— that are individually though not collectively visible; but features that only appear successively cannot cohere into the single apprehensible pattern that constitutes a face. Because the white whale's features do not exist for Ishmael in pattern, it cannot have for him that sort of prereflective meaning which comes with clarity of outline. Therefore, beyond "white whale," and "aspects of white whale," it does not exist for Ishmael as perceptual meaning.

Yet "at times" it has a meaning beyond itself that is somehow coexistent with its temporal presence, but is somehow not allegorical.

Here Frye's identification of symbols like the white whale with
Eliot's objective correlative is illuminating. Two directions of meaning are involved, inward and outward. The inward meaning is a
"focus of emotion." Against the context of Ishmael's world-view
the white whale's first meaning must be in the quality of the relation of man's consciousness to it: in, that is, how man intends it:
in what we along with Ishmael may experience confronting it in
our purposeful concern.

We do not experience that pity or sympathy we may feel confronting certain other purely temporal whales. We do not even,
strictly speaking, fear it. Earlier, Ishmael had anatomized the sort
of experience that in the end he re-creates for us:

> in the great Sperm Whale, this high and mighty god-like
> dignity inherent in the brow is so immensely amplified, that
> gazing on it, in that full front view, you feel the Deity and the
> dread powers more forcibly than in beholding any other object
> in living nature. For you see no one point precisely; not one
> distinct feature is revealed; no nose, eyes, ears, or mouth; no
> face; he has none, proper; nothing but that one broad firmament
> of a forehead, pleated with riddles; dumbly lowering with the
> doom of boats, and ships, and men.   [LXXIX]

Before the overwhelming facelessness of the whale we feel awe,
wonder, and dread: feelings which take man out of himself into a
placeless, static contemplation of futurity as the presence of an overwhelming, immensely powerful emptiness.

Possibly here is where Ishmaelean symbolism begins, and where,
for the total Ishmael, it ends. To temporal man these feelings "are"
the white whale; they are the extent of its certifiable human meaning. Ishmael has staked himself on feeling before, when he suspected
that the world is white because of his fear of invisibilities, or when
he knew that death is really an eternal absence because of men's
instinctive emotional responses to it. He has also shown us Ahab
staking everything on his pain and frustration. Thus, for Ishmael,
the white whale's meaning, like all meaning, is here finally grounded

in feeling. If the whole is both numinous and mute, the former quality is accounted for by the tension between the whale's intellectual-sensational muteness and the urgency of the feelings the whale inspires, feelings which are themselves tension. What the whale quizzically points toward is whatever such feelings will sustain. That "whatever" may be different for different people, even different for the same person at different times; and it was designed to be.

Ahab, who in his drive to *know* cannot bear the pain of their eternal ambiguity, resolves his feelings into allegory: "Evil" is what these feelings are to him, given his nature, and the whale does not contradict him. Ishmael, in the passage just quoted, associates his dread with Deity; and "God" or "agent of God" remains a possible allegorization of the white whale's meaning. For Freudian critics like Newton Arvin or Henry Murray, "the emotions Moby Dick invokes in us are the violently contradictory emotions that prevail between parent and child,"[7] so that the whale can be nothing other than (of course) "the archetypal Parent."

Like Ahab and Arvin, most critics are willing to supply designations for the whale because they feel in attenuated degree the feelings of the characters in the book; and when the ontological category of nonbeing is evoked by dread in the presence of the numinous, the mind hastens to comfort itself with an allegorical formula that will reduce to static intellectual tractability whatever formlessness it may be facing: "meditation and water are wedded for ever." The mind thinks it controls by naming. Thus the white whale "is" *to* Ishmael, and *to* Ahab, and *to* each reader. But in itself it "is" itself, and it cannot in itself be named, or structured and explained and categorized; nothingness floods through the interstices of any conceptual net designed to hold Moby Dick's essence.

Indeed, it cannot even be said that Moby Dick "is" nothingness;[8] for what Ishmael's presentation of Leviathan does by forcing us to experience an analogue of what he has experienced is force us to experience what the presence of an absence feels like. There is a sense in which Moby Dick is *not* himself until Ishmael, with his readers, has brought the creature into being. In this respect, the white whale is merely the final manifestation of much of Ishmael's strategy as a storyteller.

Ishmael is a poet who names "Moby Dick" in mockery of man's capacity to name the unnameable; but in the end Ishmael refrains from naming. It is by the sweep of his language rather more than the names it contains that he achieves his effects. He tries, by his delayed periodic sentences, his digressions, his torrent of attitudes embodied in styles, even by the boredom he sometimes evokes, to give us an impression of how existence exists through feelings. As a romantic artist, this is his truth. He creates words which try to surround the categories of life, words like those verbal nouns which, as Newton Arvin has observed, "unite the dynamism of the verb with the stasis of the substantive," blurring grammatical distinctions to express "the awareness that action and condition, movement and stasis, object and idea, are but surface aspects of one underlying reality."[9] Ishmael tries, in the words once again of Maurice Blanchot, "to evoke in the heart of the reader the same dread and the same passion which he might feel before the spectacle of cosmic creations or destructions." Ishmael's book is "a work . . . trying to compete with the forces of the universe . . . trying by its flashing variety, its torrential composition, its obscurities and ellipses, to reproduce the effect of a world grappling with the thunderbolt." Its language catches up

anyone who lets himself be taken, without his knowing where he is going or where he gets lost. It carries sparkling images which shower down with a voluptuous violence, having clarified nothing, leaving the landscape which they have illumined darker than ever from the fire which they cast upon it in vain. It attracts attention by its winding wake, it demands complete obedience, it tames a voyage which is hopeless and inescapable, and the shipwreck itself becomes no more than an insignificant accident in comparison with the cruel madness of this language which says everything and yet says nothing, finally condemned

to silence, after revelling in howls and images, by the simplicity
of its mystery.[10]

It seeks to create, in other words, a literary world of which the reader
must become a part before its final reality comes into being.

Ishmael's book is founded in his own boredom, dread, and despair.
These moods are the unity of his consciousness, and of his book.
They are the correlatives of his book's "objects," and as moods they
are neither frivolous nor fleeting. Certain romantic philosophies
would hold that they are nothing less than ontological: they are
not something we have, but something we are. Whether or not that
is true, *Moby Dick* tries to persuade us to become these moods in
order to discover their meanings within ourselves; it does so by
submerging the initially amusing character Ishmael into the ambiguous voice of the narrator, whose feelings in relation to his
strange world provide analogues for ours. Melville once wrote to
Hawthorne that in *Moby Dick* he had produced a wicked book; perhaps Melville's book is "wicked" not so much because of its unortho-
dox attitudes, but because it has found literary means through which
it can proselytize with some success for its heresies.

Ishmael goes to sea in endless repetition to create meaning out of
emptiness. For him, there is no Bible to reveal Truth. The only
experienced truth is human truth, and that is dependent on each man
living out his own vision. Ishmael is a mental traveler who accepts
with minimal illusions and defenses his human condition in that
world of experience to which, like the lone figure floating on a coffin
at the end, humanity seems abandoned.

References

Phenomenological

Bachelard, Gaston, *L'Eau et les rêves,* Paris, 1942.
———, *La Psychanalyse du feu,* Paris, 1939.
Sartre, Jean-Paul, *The Emotions,* trans. Bernard Frechtman, New York, 1948.
Schmitt, Richard, "In Search of Phenomenology," *Review of Metaphysics, 15,* No. 3 (1962).
Spiegelberg, Herbert, *The Phenomenological Movement,* 2 vols. The Hague, 1960.
Van den Berg, J. H., *The Phenomenological Approach to Psychiatry,* Springfield, 1955.

Philosophical

James, William, *Selected Papers on Philosophy,* New York, 1947.
Kierkegaard, Søren, *The Concept of Dread,* Princeton, 1948.
———, *Concluding Unscientific Postscript,* Princeton, 1944.
———, *Fear and Trembling and The Sickness unto Death,* New York, 1954.
———, *Repetition,* Princeton, 1946.

Critical

Arvin, Newton, *Herman Melville,* New York, 1950.
Auden, W. H., *The Enchafèd Flood,* London, 1951.
Blanchot, Maurice, *Faux-Pas,* 10th ed. Paris, 1943.
Borton, John, *Herman Melville: The Philosophical Implications of Literary Technique in Moby Dick,* Amherst, 1961.
Braswell, William, *Melville's Religious Thought,* Durham, 1943.
Cambon, Glauco, "Ishmael and the Problem of Formal Discontinuities in *Moby Dick,*" *Modern Language Notes,* 76 (1961).

Cook, Charles H., Jr., "Ahab's 'Intolerable Allegory,'" *Boston University Studies in English, 1,* 1955–56.

Fiedler, Leslie, *Love and Death in the American Novel,* New York, 1960.

Frye, Northrop, *Anatomy of Criticism,* Princeton, 1957.

Hoffman, Daniel, *Form and Fable in American Fiction,* New York, 1961.

Horsford, Howard C., "The Design of the Argument in *Moby Dick,*" *Modern Fiction Studies, 8,* No. 3 (Autumn 1962).

Leyda, Jay, *The Melville Log,* 2 vols. New York, 1951.

Mason, Ronald, *The Spirit above the Dust,* London, 1951.

Matthiessen, F. O., *American Renaissance,* New York, 1941.

Miller, J. Hillis, *The Disappearance of God,* Cambridge, 1963.

Mumford, Lewis, *Herman Melville,* New York, 1929.

Murray, Henry A., "In Nomine Diaboli," in *Moby Dick Centennial Essays,* ed. Mansfield, Luther, and Tyrus Hillway.

Percival, M. O., *A Reading of Moby Dick,* Chicago, 1950.

Pochmann, Henry A., *German Culture in America,* Madison, 1957.

Poulet, Georges, *Studies in Human Time,* New York, 1959.

Rosenberry, Edward H., *Melville and the Comic Spirit,* Cambridge, 1955.

Rourke, Constance, *American Humor,* New York, 1931.

Sealts, Merton M., Jr., "Melville's Reading: A Check-List of Books Owned and Borrowed," *Harvard Library Bulletin, 2, 3, 4, 6* (1948, 1949, 1950, 1952).

Seelye, John, "The Golden Navel: The Cabalism of Ahab's Doubloon," *Nineteenth Century Fiction, 14,* No. 4 (1960).

Shulman, Robert, "The Serious Function of Melville's Phallic Jokes," *American Literature, 33,* No. 2 (1961).

Sundermann, Karl-Heinz, *Herman Melvilles Gedankengut,* Berlin, 1937.

Thompson, Lawrance, *Melville's Quarrel with God,* Princeton, 1952.

Wheeler, Otis, "Humor in *Moby Dick:* Two Problems," *American Literature, 29,* No. 2 (1957).

NOTES

Introduction

1. J. Hillis Miller, *The Disappearance of God* (Cambridge, 1963), p. vii.

2. Northrop Frye, *Anatomy of Criticism* (Princeton, 1957), p. 77.

3. If all this can seem to deny the historical fact that Melville did make most of the mistakes, and that they *are* mistakes, it need not do so. For my purposes in what follows in the text, I do not have to maintain so rigidly formal a separation between Ishmael and Melville, though I did want to record the extent to which it could be insisted upon if only because Ishmael's presence as *storyteller* will be crucial later, not to absolve Melville but to make sense of Ishmael in larger perspectives. Thus, the literary fact consequent upon the historical fact may more accurately be stated as follows: Ishmael is first of all a consciousness. As consciousness, it is Ishmael's consciousness comprehending its own content and Melville's consciousness comprehending the total Ishmael. It makes no difference to my purposes whether that compound consciousness be called "Ishmael," "Melville," or "Ishmael-Melville." Whatever its name, it will show precisely the unified characteristics of any consciousness disclosing itself in different modes, and the sorts of unity a consciousness will show phenomenologically easily cut across any such boundaries. For convenience, because *Moby Dick* does so, I will call the consciousness in question "Ishmael."

An excellent discussion of the problem of Ishmael's total presence from the point of view of *Moby Dick's* modal displacements from narrative to drama is to be found in Glauco Cambon's "Ishmael and the Problem of Formal Discontinuities in *Moby Dick*," *Modern Language Notes*, 76 (1961), which corroborates my argument here and elsewhere (especially in Chapter 6). Cambon finds a tripartite structurally significant occurrence of the dramatically immediate episodes, which find part of their justification in narrator-Ishmael's attempts "to bring home to his audience the poignancy of some particular experience relived now" (p. 522), attempts which "embody the natural movement of memory striving to recapture lost actuality" (ibid.). Ishmael is a "conjuring" (p. 523) narrator imaginatively reconstituting characters he once knew; his "memory modulates into imagination, and we share the experience of creation in progress" (ibid.). For Cambon as for myself, Ishmael is an artist who both tells us of, and struggles to understand, his crucial experiences.

4. My categories are baldly appropriated from *The Phenomenological Approach to Psychiatry* by J. H. Van den Berg (Springfield, 1955). In this clear, quite nontechnical book, these generally Heideggerian concepts are presented with many concrete illustrations to clarify for American psychologists the ideas used by European phenomenological psychology to understand individual *Lebenswelten* (the word is Edmund Husserl's). From my point of view the advantage of the categories is that they can order the Ishmaelean consciousness without prior commitment on the part of my reader to my "system." That is, the concepts can be provisionally accepted because they are primarily existential categories rather than metaphysical ones (such as id, superego, and so forth); the reader may not believe that there is such a thing as a superego, but he must be a hard case indeed to deny the usefulness of "time," "body," "world," and "others" as classifying entities. Van den Berg deals at length with the relationships of the categories to each other: in brief, "world" is "the materialization of our subjectivity" (p. 32)—i.e. we encounter ourselves in our perceptions of the universe; our bodies relate to the experienced world, gracefully or awkwardly, in a "continuous conversation" (p. 44); our relations with others become realized "in the physiognomy, the vicinity or the distance, of world and body" (p. 57). In sum, within human consciousness, each of the first three categories implies the others. The fourth category is fundamental for the other three, since they have the ground of their being in the subjective experience of *time*.

5. The assertion that a work of art has unity is perhaps still too unexamined an accolade of formal criticism, and its opposite too easy a libel. One implication of phenomenological commentary (as it is of psychological, stylistic, and synoptic commentary) is that even the most expansively exuberant romantic art will show unity under scrutiny that expects to find it. Indeed, a glance at the history of criticism confirms that any work of art sufficiently intense and interesting to be admired despite its apparent lack of unity will eventually find a critic disposed and able to demonstrate that it really does hang together; and because unity is in the mind of the observer as well as in the observed object, its presence or absence says very little about necessary literary quality: bad art can be as unified as good art, depending on whose intelligence is addressing it. As Leibniz once demonstrated and modern science continues to demonstrate, even chaoses can be mathematically charted into patterns, but this fact proves the objective laws of nature no more than the uncovering of unsuspected unity proves the objective laws of art; though the demonstration itself does perhaps say some-

thing about one pervasive tendency of the human mind, as Henry Adams, for one, well knew.

Chapter 1

1. However, there is no way of knowing. Sundermann's conclusion is opposed by the equally weighty Henry A. Pochmann, who, in his monumental *German Culture in America* (Madison, 1957), finds Melville intimately acquainted with and influenced by Kant, to the point of being inclined to read *Moby Dick* as a kind of allegory of Kant's pure reason always (as it is embodied in Ahab) unable to know matter, and *Pierre* as an allegory operating on the stage of the moral concerns of Kant's practical reason (pp. 437–38). Pochmann's readings are perhaps too linear to be convincing as he states them; yet, divorced from their undemonstrable basis in intellectual history, and restated in more tentatively undogmatic terms, they could be more illuminating. Indeed, a history of ideas argument too definitely formulated is finally likely to prove elusive: Howard C. Horsford in a recent article ("The Design of the Argument in *Moby Dick,*" *Modern Fiction Studies, 8,* No. 3, Autumn 1962) stakes his excellent reading of *Moby Dick* on the premise that the book's epistemology comes from David Hume—but Kant would do as well, of course, to justify Horsford's feeling that the novel represents the experience of a "millennially old tradition viewed in a terrifying new perspective, of sensing faith and conviction disintegrate, so to speak, before one's eyes" (p. 237). Kant has the additional advantage of making mind and matter less unconnected than they are in Hume, an advantage in *Moby Dick,* at least, because there mind has a great deal to do with how matter appears and can even to some extent coerce the manifestations of matter, as in Ahab's relation to the whale, ship, and crew (to be discussed in Chapter 4, below). I myself should not care to stake very much on precisely where Melville found his ideas, since versions of them were intellectually ubiquitous in the nineteenth century, and he always rang important changes on their originators' statements of them in any case.

2. *Melville's Religious Thought* (Durham, 1943), p. 14.

3. Melville's journal entry for October 12, 1849, quoted in *The Melville Log,* edited by Jay Leyda (New York, 1951), *1,* 319. This is only one of many entries in which Adler suggests Kant to Melville.

4. J.-P. Sartre, *The Emotions,* trans. Bernard Frechtman (New York, 1948), p. 52.

5. Ibid., p. 75.

6. "On a Certain Blindness in Human Beings," reprinted in *Selected Papers on Philosophy* (New York, 1947), p. 15.

7. Van den Berg, p. 31.

8. The phrase is Melville's in reference to the tenor of his conversations with Hawthorne around the time of *Moby Dick's* composition; it can be found in his letter to Hawthorne of June 29, 1851 (quoted in Leyda, *1*, 415). My concluding assertion that the "ontological heroics" of *Moby Dick* take place on a stage of subjectivity has been made before in Melville criticism. The second epigraph to this chapter records Edward H. Rosenberry's passing observation that "on all questions of significance the prior question becomes: Seen by whom, in what mood, and in what light?" (*Melville and the Comic Spirit*, Cambridge, 1955, p. 116). F. O. Matthiessen, also, in *American Renaissance* (New York, 1941) notes that "Melville had gone farther than Emerson in his realization that what you find in nature, whether you consider a phenomenon angelic or diabolic, depends—as Coleridge knew in the 'Ode to Dejection'—greatly on your own mood" (p. 406). What Coleridge knew—"we receive but what we give, / And in our life alone does Nature live"—Melville knew quite as thoroughly, and Coleridge as well as George Adler, Kant, and Emerson may have been his formal teachers. Other critics besides Matthiessen and Rosenberry have made the point, but if the point really is well taken, it becomes literally of fundamental importance to take subjectivity into account in reading Melville; and though most Melville critics do, by and large they do so explicitly only when necessary to affirm or deny some particular point in some particular book. My attempt here is to take it into systematic account throughout one book. (A pamphlet by John Borton—evidently an Amherst undergraduate at the time he wrote it —entitled *Herman Melville: The Philosophical Implications of Literary Technique*, Amherst, 1961, promises in its title rather more than it delivers. Borton's actual concern is to derive a philosophy of action [p. 7] from *Moby Dick* and "Billy Budd," and he has little to say on more general matters of the philosophical implications.)

Chapter 2

1. The delicately Rabelaisian chapter called "The Cassock" may be understood in the context of a masculine world. In it, the mincer "in the full canonicals of his calling" becomes an animate phallus, resembling the idol "found in the secret groves of Queen Maachah." The idol was an emblem of masculine power, worshiped in fertility rituals that existed partly to petition the gods for good crop yields. Here, a living man now animates the power of the idol, and his function as mincer is analogous to that of the ancient idol: he is to cut the thinnest possible slices of blubber so that the quantity of oil they will yield is "considerably increased, besides perhaps

improving in quality." He is the practical, self-help sort of idol likely to appear in the masculine world of the book. The vaguely locker-room leer of the chapter's tone is also part of the masculine world which yearns for the absent femininity that is needed to complete it. The *structural* function and meaning of the chapter, however, is doubtless to be found in its concluding blasphemy: the mincer becomes an obscene archbishop presiding over the black mass of the immediately succeeding try-works chapter, the experience of which inverts Ishmael. The mincer thereby makes explicitly ritualistic one of the inversions and reversals that celebrate the approach of the white whale (to be considered in Chapter 6, below).

2. The point has been made in philosophical language by Søren Kierkegaard, among others: If "truth is defined . . . empirically, as the conformity of thought with being . . . it is . . . important carefully to note what is meant by being. . . . If being . . . is understood as empirical being, truth is at once transformed into a *desideratum,* and everything must be understood in terms of becoming; for the empirical object is unfinished and the existing cognitive spirit is itself in the process of becoming. Thus the truth becomes an approximation whose beginning cannot be posited absolutely precisely because the conclusion is lacking, the effect of which is retroactive." See *Concluding Unscientific Postscript* (Princeton, 1944), p. 169.

3. White birds accompany the Pequod to its rendezvous with the white whale; a bird steals Ahab's hat, stripping from him the last man-made protection for his brain against the full power of the sun and wind (Charles Olson and F. O. Matthiessen have noted the analogue of Lear's nakedness); a bird steals the ship's wind vane, perhaps to lessen Ahab's measure of control over the power of the winds; and a "bird of heaven, with archangelic shrieks" (an albatross, the prototype bird of heaven in a footnote to chapter XLII, also has "archangel wings"), tries to snatch a trophy from the sinking Pequod, but (if it were truly an emissary from the sky gods) rather bumbles its mission.

4. Fedallah appears as a primal man in passages like the one in chapter L: "He was such a creature as civilized, domestic people in the temperate zone only see in their dreams, and that but dimly; but the like of whom now and then glide among the unchanging Asiatic communities, especially the Oriental isles to the east of the continent—those insulated, immemorial, unalterable countries, which even in these modern days still preserve much of the ghostly aboriginalness of earth's primal generations, when the memory of the first man was a distinct recollection, and all men his descendants, unknowing whence he came, eyed each other as real phantoms, and asked of the sun and the moon why they were created and to what end . . ."

5. The Pequod begins her voyage at noon, but it instantly becomes night

as far as the book is concerned: "At last the anchor was up, the sails were set, and off we glided. It was a short, cold Christmas; and as the short northern day merged into night, we found ourselves almost broad upon the wintry ocean, whose freezing spray cased us in ice, as in polished armor" (XXII); the next chapter reiterates the nighttime character of the journey's outset: "When on that shivering winter's night, the Pequod thrust her vindictive bows into the cold malicious waves . . ."

6. That Ishmael actually never ends his restlessness is merely asserted here, but will be demonstrated, I hope adequately, in Chapter 6.

7. The passage is quoted more extensively on page 22, above.

8. Madness may be called static because it is typologically rigid: viewed clinically, psychotics run truer to type than sane men. In a curious way, they are more predictable (Pip's refrain on cowardice is like a broken phonograph record; Ahab's madness is explicitly a monomania, and when he says "Ahab is for ever Ahab" [CXXXIV], by asserting his immutability he is unintentionally characterizing his madness as well as arguing for predestination). The ambiguity of the stasis of madness is that while madness is typologically rigid, it is also spontaneous: Pip's obsession with cowardice is predictable, but his "crazy-witty" insights are not, nor are Ahab's variously improvised tactics to inflame the crew. Both rigid and fluid, perhaps the inclusively dialectical character of madness is part of what gives it its conventionally privileged access to the truths of Being.

9. Ishmael suggests that its character is heartless, mindless, chaotic creativity, but since only *Pip* has actually returned from those depths and does not report intelligibly on them, perhaps Ishmael's negative capability here does not quite qualify him to be "an author from the dead" (CX); and his suggestion, though highly plausible, has perhaps no greater ultimate validity than any other shrewd inference from phenomenal characteristics on the temporal side of eternity.

Chapter 3

1. The examples are from Van den Berg, pp. 38–39.

2. As in the largest sense the movements of Ishmael's body express *him:* his willed vocation of traveler comprehends a major part of his identity.

Chapter 4

1. Matthiessen, p. 426.

2. The pronouns signify decreasing degrees of personal engagement with the other. The distinction is taken from Martin Buber.

3. Matthiessen, p. 126.

4. Ibid.

5. Ibid., p. 128.

6. Lawrance Thompson in *Melville's Quarrel with God* (Princeton, 1952) makes a related point about Father Mapple's sermon by emphasizing what follows it: Ishmael joins Queequeg in the grotesque worship of Queequeg's idol (pp. 163–64). Thompson also finds Mapple to be burlesqued, but only by the symbolic action he notes and by certain doctrinal statements in the sermon wherein he finds hidden anti-Christian double meanings: e.g. "To preach the Truth to the face of Falsehood" insults the Christian reader, who is himself Falsehood. Mapple's own rhetoric Thompson admires.

7. "Common vitality" I construe to mean in context that vitality or animating principle which is both soul and mind ("the mind does not exist unless leagued with the soul") rather than a vague ordinary vitality which would be out of keeping with Ishmael's labored attempt at precision here.

8. For example, those in chapters XLI, XLIV, and XLVI.

9. M. O. Percival in *A Reading of Moby Dick* (Chicago, 1950) was the first of many to suggest that the Parsee could be understood as "the subtly maddened part of Ahab's mind" (p. 41).

10. W. H. Auden, with Percival a Kierkegaardian reader of *Moby Dick,* sees Ahab as a religious hero, negatively manifested, in his book *The Enchafèd Flood* (London, 1951). I am indebted to both Auden and Percival in this analysis of Ahab, though more for attitudes than specific arguments.

11. Auden's definition in Kierkegaardian terms of the religious hero is similar:

> Religious authority . . . arises . . . from a relation to truth. But the religious definition of truth is . . . that it is absolute. The religious hero is one who is committed to anything with absolute passion, i.e., to him it is the absolute truth, his god. The stress is so strongly on the absolute that though he may be passionately related to what, ethically . . . is false, he is a religious hero and has religious authority over the one who is lukewarmly or dispassionately related to what is true.
>
> [p. 86]

12. If God's actions in the Old Testament are any evidence, human ethics do not exist within God's realm. God is absolute; for Him there can be no *necessary* consequences no matter what He chooses to do. Existentially, ethics are pragmatic means for accomplishing ends; divinely, ethics would be superfluous because God accomplishes His will without any such means: He says, "Let there be light," and there is.

13. Ahab's fire speech is also discussed on page 91, below.

14. These formulas may well be ironic, but this seems to be a case of that

sort of Ishmaelean irony (discussed below, pages 135–37) about which one cannot be *sure*. Out of context, the words seem to imply their opposite in order to mock Ahab's pride; but in context, Ahab has by no means yet demonstrated hybris worthy of Ishmael's scorn: they merely serve to indicate Ishmael's recollection (occasioned by the sight of Ahab seated on a whale-bone tripod stool) of "old Norse times" and "the thrones of the sea-loving Danish kings." Perhaps the hyperbole is self-directed irony as much as directed against Ahab: perhaps the irony undercuts that part of Ishmael which must see Ahab in so exalted a way—undercuts, that is, that part of himself which admires Ahab's self-willed certainty enough to make of it an heroic attribute even though he suspects a fatal error in that certainty. The direction of the irony, in any case, does not seem univocal.

15. Some philosophers, most notably perhaps Martin Heidegger, suggest that people who speak different languages experience different worlds. (The idea is part of the common ground between European phenomenology and the philosophy of the British analytic school; I might add that many American academicians will be familiar with the issue of language's radical participation in fact from the poetry and poetics of Wallace Stevens, or from the writings in linguistics of Benjamin Lee Whorf.) Such a formulation is at best controversial, and will not be insisted upon here. But it may be safe to assert that in *Moby Dick* the Shakespearean aura around Ahab's speech is of a piece with the kind of world he experiences, and that that world is of a greater range and depth than, say, Flask's. For a discussion of the formulation cited at the beginning of this note see Richard Schmitt, "In Search of Phenomenology," *Review of Metaphysics, 15,* No. 3 (1962).

16. The tendency of much otherwise excellent Melville criticism finally to condemn Ahab often involves a prior reduction of the sort of stature granted Ahab by Ishmael's presentation of him. But surely problematic heroes who escape clear ethical evaluation are not that unprecedented in literature even before the romantic movement. Consider all the literary figures who embody great force of spirit instead of unambiguous virtue; whose abnormally passionate aspirations are defeated by the gods, or merely by the cyclical everydayness of the world; whose violations of common decency are somehow part of their heroism, which is finally an affront to common decency. If Ahab evokes from Stubb, and from some readers, an un-Christian respect for his inviolable integrity of purpose, Ahab's admirers are part of a tradition that goes back at least as far as the stoics, who also valued individual honor even when it went against the good of the community. (That part of Ishmael which is constrained to present Ahab as a hero, despite what his ethical knowledge tells him, *is* stoic; a reason for the affinity is suggested on page 125, below.)

17. ". . . comme si la liberté et les impulsions personnelles, beaucoup plus que le mouvement d'un mécanisme inéluctable, étaient les vraies voies de la fatalité." See "Le Secret de Melville," *Faux-Pas* (10th ed. Paris, 1943), p. 285.

18. Two examples of dialogue will serve to illustrate the simple point meant here:

> "The oil in the hold is leaking, sir. We must up Burtons and break out." [Ahab is incredulous.] "Either do that, sir, or waste in one day more oil than we may make good in a year. What we come twenty thousand miles to get is worth saving, sir."
> "So it is, so it is; if we get it."
> "I was speaking of the oil in the hold, sir."
> "And I was not speaking or thinking of that at all. Begone!"   [CIX]

> [Ahab:] "How the soot flies! This must be the remainder the Greek [Prometheus] made the African of. Carpenter, when [the blacksmith] is through with that buckle, tell him to forge a pair of steel shoulder-blades; there's a pedlar aboard with a crushing pack."
> "Sir?"
> "Hold; while Prometheus is about it, I'll order a complete man . . ." etc.   [CVIII]

19. The comparison of Ishmael with the ancient mariner is no more than a tentative suggestion here; it will be developed further near the end of Chapter 6, below.

Chapter 5

1. Here I paraphrase Blake: "Prophets in the modern sense of the word, have never existed. Jonah was no prophet in the modern sense, for his prophecy of Ninevah failed. Every honest man is a Prophet; he utters his opinion both of private and public matters. Thus: If you go on So, the result is So. He never says, such a thing shall happen let you do what you will. A Prophet is a Seer, not an Arbitrary Dictator." *The Complete Writings of William Blake,* ed. Geoffrey Keynes (London, 1957), p. 392.

2. Natural teleology ("Isn't it wonderful how Mother Nature gives the giraffe a long neck to reach those upper branches") is only visible to some-one who assumes it in the first place. A giraffe's neck can with equal validity be seen as utterly absurd, doubtless presently useful to the giraffe, but no explanation of why the giraffe is not a rhinoceros.

3. It will be recalled that this chapter tries to establish the credibility of Ahab's death: "With reference to the whaling scene shortly to be described,

as well as for the better understanding of all similar scenes elsewhere presented, I have here to speak of the magical, sometimes horrible whale-line." Ishmael explains the complex and dangerous working of the line, then adds: "Perhaps a very little thought will now enable you to account for those repeated whaling disasters—some few of which are casually chronicled—of this man or that man being taken out of the boat by the line, and lost."

4. Ishmael becomes Ahab's bowsman, as the epilogue explains, only after Fedallah had been swept overboard. Normally he belongs to Starbuck's boat, as is noted in chapter XLIX.

5. When Ahab says, "Now, then, be the prophet and fulfiller one" (XXXVII), he is raging against the fulfilled prophecy that he would lose a leg; and after swearing this, he goes on to assert his superiority of stature over that of the gods, who are merely "cricket-players" and "pugilists." His reaction is by no means a necessary one, even for a man of integrity; Father Mapple, for instance, would see predestination as *adding* to human dignity because it is a direct influx of the divine, and gives to man religious meaning: it is evidence of God's concern.

6. In chapter XXVI Ishmael, trying to justify aesthetically his transformation of Starbuck (and, of course, Ahab) into nobly "dark" actors in an epic tragedy even though their basis in actuality was something less, argues that his version of their dignity of stature is true at least to their ideal essence. Man in the mass may seem "detestable," but ideal Man is "noble," a "grand and glowing creature," with an "abounding dignity which has no robed investiture." Even "knaves, fools, and murderers" may hide shining ideality behind their particular human blemishes.

7. The Cato reference may suggest intellectual inconsistency by analogy: though Cato had lived for a free state, and saw its death as the signal for his own, his suicide is not unambiguously stoic—his circumscribed philosophy was to act out of present duty without regard to the future, but just before he killed himself (so the legend goes) he chose to read Plato's dialogue on the immortality of the soul. His may have been a deathbed conversion *from* stoicism manifesting itself in a stoic act.

8. The passage was analyzed above, pages 16–17.

9. That Ishmael is a self-given name will be argued in Chapter 6. The New Englanders and Nantucketers of actuality knew their Bibles well enough not to name children Ishmael or Ahab.

10. Georges Poulet, *Studies in Human Time,* trans. Elliot Coleman (Harper Torchbooks, 1959), p. 341. The appendix entitled "Time and American Writers" does not appear in the first hard-cover edition published in 1956 by the Johns Hopkins Press.

11. See above, page 21.

Chapter 6

1. For example, the famous passage in chapter XCIV wherein Ishmael says he has perceived that man must shift "his conceit of attainable felicity; not placing it anywhere in the intellect or the fancy; but in the wife, the heart, the bed, the table, the saddle, the fire-side, the country; now that I have perceived all this, I am ready to squeeze case eternally." But retiring to the country is just what Ishmael does not do; Ishmael is not Melville.

2. "Literally" may seem too strong a way of putting it, since both the new Webster's *Third International* and the *OED* list "to bore" in the sense of to cause boredom as of unknown etymology; but the *OED* in its discussion of "bore," *sb.* 2 (the malady of *ennui* or anyone who suffers from or, along with any thing, causes it) suggests that the first sense of the substantive ("that which is bored, a hole caused by boring") is "apparently the source of the other senses, and of the verb itself." The *OED* is unable to trace the derivation of the modern (about 1750) malaise from the Old Norse "bore hole" which is the source of the first substantive it thinks may underlie all other senses. Though linguistically there may be a problem here, phenomenologically there is none: to feel bored is to feel hollowed out, therefore empty.

3. One of the most recent extended analyses of Ishmael's waking-dream, that of Daniel Hoffman in *Form and Fable in American Fiction* (New York, 1961), treats the episode psychoanalytically and finds in it a key to Ishmael's inhibition of his "expression of Eros" (p. 266). Leslie Fiedler in *Love and Death in the American Novel* (New York, 1960) finds on pages 535–36 that, because of the "hand," the association with maternal punishment, and the fact that Ishmael will never "rise again," the dream is a guilt-ridden masturbation fantasy. Chacun à son goût.

4. One of Kierkegaard's definitions of *Angst* (English has no single equivalent that will span the phenomenon's affective range) is "the reality of freedom as a potentiality before this freedom has realized itself" (*The Concept of Dread*, trans. Walter Lowrie, Princeton, 1944, p. 38; I have slightly altered Lowrie's translation here to give a clearer sense of the Danish). When we dread, we are forced to contemplate the inexplicability of a potentiality that threatens our present existence; yet as *freedom,* this potentiality is strangely attractive, a "sympathetic antipathy" (ibid.). The same is true at the dilute level of anxiety: for example, I am offered a well-paid job doing something I like in Des Moines, but to take this job means uprooting myself from my less well-paid, less interesting job in New York; but New York is New York and Des Moines is Des Moines. If the subjective

values balance out, I am in neither New York nor Des Moines but a state of indecisive anxiety. I have been faced with the freedom and potentiality of my own nonbeing.

5. There is a famous passage in Kierkegaard's experimental novel *Repetition* (Princeton, 1946) that expresses part of Ishmael's point in a nicely Ishmaelean tone of self-ironic banter: "One sticks one's finger into the soil to tell by the smell in what land one is: I stick my finger into existence—it smells of nothing. Where am I? Who am I? How came I here? What is this thing called the world? What does this word mean? Who is it that has lured me into the thing, and now leaves me there? Who am I? How did I come into the world? Why was I not consulted, why not made acquainted with its manners and customs . . .? How did I obtain an interest in this big enterprise they call reality? Why should I have an interest in it? Is it not a voluntary concern? And if I am to be compelled to take part in it, where is the director? I should like to make a remark to him. Is there no director? Whither shall I turn with my complaint? . . . What is a deceiver? Does not Cicero say that a deceiver can be found out by asking the question *cui bono?* I allow everyone to ask, and I ask everyone . . ."   [Pp. 114–15]

6. See pages 16–17, above.

7. The passage is quoted at length above, page 33.

8. The words come from the first sentence of chapter XLII: "What the white whale was to Ahab, has been hinted; what, at times, he was to me, as yet remains unsaid." The "at times" suggests that Moby Dick's "white" meaning governs Ishmael's apprehension of the whale discontinuously. One implication of this will be suggested later in the text.

9. Similarly, the doubloon, "the white whale's talisman" (XCIX), is "yon ratifying sun" (XXXVI); Moby Dick's home-seas near the equator resemble an "immeasurable burning-glass" ("the sky looks lacquered; clouds there are none; the horizon floats; and this nakedness of unrelieved radiance is as the insufferable splendors of God's throne," CXVIII); Moby Dick is encountered at the "Season-on-the-Line" where, "for several years, [he] had been periodically descried, lingering in those waters for awhile, as the sun, in its annual round, loiters for a predicted interval in any one sign of the Zodiac" (XLIV); "Aye, breach your last to the sun," says Ahab on the second day of the chase.

10. If the book is equally divided in two by the number of its pages, the second half has twenty-five chapters more than the first half.

11. As M. O. Percival has noted in *A Reading of Moby Dick,* p. 16; and W. H. Auden in *The Enchafèd Flood,* p. 114.

12. Alfred Kazin, in one of the best short pieces written on *Moby Dick*

(his introduction to the Riverside edition), has said that Melville gives us the whale's view of things. If we remember that because of the separation of its eyes a whale's vision is composed of two distinct pictures, between which all is "profound darkness and nothingness" (LXXIV), we see the literal truth of Kazin's remark: through Ishmael's consciousness we perceive the world in dialectical images, with darkness and nothingness between.

13. Charles H. Cook, Jr., in "Ahab's 'Intolerable Allegory,'" *Boston University Studies in English, 1* (1955–56), finds that Ahab dies because he allegorizes and Ishmael lives because he symbolizes. Cook's distinction seems to me valid, though his conclusion, I think, moralizes beyond what the total book will support. The point is developed later in the text.

14. "I mean, sir," Ishmael goes on, "the same ancient Catholic Church to which you and I, and Captain Peleg there, and Queequeg here, and all of us, and every mother's son and soul of us belong; the great and everlasting First Congregation of this whole worshipping world; we all belong to that; only some of us cherish some queer crotchets noways touching the grand belief; in *that* we all join hands."

15. There is another possibility, of course: the literal implication of the phrase, that Bulkington sleeps with Ishmael. This would posit an Ishmael out of Leslie Fiedler's worst moments who would rather not confess under his own name because, in part, of the implied homosexuality of several of his experiences. Despite the incredulity such a suggestion may raise, the grammatical and referential possibility *is* there, and for those who want it to be it can subvert the content of the Bulkington episode in ways similar to the ones soon to be discussed in the text.

16. As in the case of Narcissus, who makes his image mean a being distinctly someone else in the water, and thereby clarifies it beyond what it is. The whale, however, with no face, cannot be given normal human perceptional meaning.

This assertion, in various formulations, is by now a commonplace of many modern psychologies, but it has been demonstrated most convincingly, perhaps, by Gestaltists. An elementary demonstration is the famous duck-rabbit drawing: the "duck" faces left, the "rabbit" right. Because it is hard to perceive the outline without making it "mean" discontinuously one or the other animal, it can be concluded that for man, normally, objects hardly exist except insofar as they already have meaning, which is conferred in the very act of perception. Perception, in short, is really apperception.

17. *Fear and Trembling and The Sickness unto Death* (New York, 1954), p. 148.

18. I offer this analysis as an alternative solution to the one proposed by

Otis Wheeler in "Humor in *Moby Dick:* Two Problems," *American Literature, 29,* No. 2 (1957). Wheeler notes the inconsistency and finds the
reason for it in Melville's changing conception of the book as he rewrote
it, Ishmael changing in the process from a comic character to a philosopher.
Of course, a great many of the coarser jokes are in the revised sections, and
the entire problem disappears if the inconsistency is more apparent than real.

19. The joke, current on the Eastern seaboard about ten years ago, involves an extremely long, dead-pan build-up that stresses the sanctity and
sincerity of a Hindu holy man on a high mountaintop who after years of
contemplating his navel decides that it ought to be possible to unscrew it,
and that if he were to do so he would at last have all the final answers. In
some versions of the story a golden screwdriver descends from the sky to the
mountaintop (the story is full of archetypes); the mystic grasps it and un-
screws his navel, only to have his ass fall off. In an odd way the "fundamental"
moral of the story fits as a possible answer to Pip's question, though the
tone, here as elsewhere, does not. That the joke existed in the nineteenth
century, a version of it in print in 1855, is noted by John Seelye in "The
Golden Navel: The Cabalism of Ahab's Doubloon," in *Nineteenth Century
Fiction, 14,* No. 4 (1960). Since jokes get into print considerably after their
oral currency, it is hard not to believe that Melville knew it.

20. Thompson, p. 218.

21. Robert Shulman in "The Serious Function of Melville's Phallic
Jokes," *American Literature, 33,* No. 2 (1961) finds that such jokes "help
Ishmael satirize the norms of the respectable community and to assert the
value of independent creativity and a socially defiant creator" (p. 194).
Shulman's Lawrentian-Freudian bias leads him to assert but not demonstrate
that phallicism meant creativity to Melville. I would agree that such meaning
may very well have been part of Melville's timidly Rabelaisian intention,
but forced as he was in nineteenth-century America to conceal most of his
obscenities, these do not emerge from the book with sufficient force to be
felt as in themselves of positive value; instead, the more hidden ones make
the reader uneasy if he notices them at all, while the less hidden ones may
be funny enough to help nullify serious meaning where they occur, but
they do not seem to me bold enough to assert phallic countervalues. Shulman's argument differs from mine less in essence than emphasis, however:
I feel that in their destruction of meaning is the major force of their creativity
—if you destroy established values you have a chance, like Ishmael, to be
born again from chaos and live your new life facing without mediation
the leprous world: Melville is pre-Lawrence, not post.

22. Ishmael suggests sexual play on the word "harpoon" in the chapter
called "Fast-Fish and Loose-Fish," in which it is recounted that a "gentleman

had originally harpooned" a lady, but "abandoned her on the seas of life" because of her "plunging viciousness" and "a subsequent gentleman re-harpooned her." The Shulman article cited in the preceding footnote documents many such usages.

23. See especially Flaubert's letter of January 16, 1852, to Louise Colet. It appears on p. 125 of Francis Steegmuller's edition of the *Selected Letters* (Anchor Books, 1957). The letters on pages 139, 148, and 253 are also startlingly parallel to Melville's thought as Ishmael reflects it.

Chapter 7

1. The phrase actually comes from Ishmael's meditation on the meaning of Father Mapple's pulpit, but it prepares for the later, less explicit, allegorization of the Pequod in chapter XXVII: "Yet now, federated along one keel, what a set these Isolatoes were! An Anarchasis Clootz deputation from all the isles of the sea, and all the ends of the earth, accompanying Old Ahab in the Pequod to lay the world's grievances before that bar from which not very many of them ever come back."

2. S. T. Coleridge, *The Complete Works,* ed. W. G. T. Shedd (New York, 1884), 1, 437–38.

3. Newton Arvin, *Herman Melville* (New York, 1950), p. 166.

4. Twentieth-century criticism, at any rate, has begun to rehabilitate allegory by showing that nineteenth-century criticism had been unjust to the concept in many ways, one of which was a reversal of the true priority of interest in vehicle and idea. Yet even modern criticism tends to see allegory as something self-evidently and wholly distinct from, say, symbolism, when it probably is not. For even if we read a white whale as Evil, as soon as we question ourselves what we *really* mean by Evil everything falls apart and dissolves back into something like symbolism again. In other words, what still preserves allegory as a separate category of literature designating more than certain products of a particular era of consciously formulated theory and practice is that modern interpreters (and writers) of allegory too often do not question what *they* mean by their allegorical "meanings."

5. The possibility that Ishmael is a bad (because unclear) maker of allegory is discounted in the simple charity advocated above, pages 4–5.

6. As Ishmael's alternative speculations suggest: "Whether fagged by the three days' running chase . . . or whether it was some latent deceitfulness and malice in him; whichever was true, the White Whale's way now began to abate . . ." (CXXXV).

7. Arvin, p. 173. Henry A. Murray's "In Nomine Diaboli," reprinted in *Moby Dick Centennial Essays,* ed. Hillway and Mansfield (Dallas, 1953),

agrees with Arvin's reading. Since Murray is a professional psychologist at Harvard as well as a Melville scholar, the reading can doubtless stand as the official eclectic-Freudian one.

8. Ronald Mason in his biographical and critical study of Melville, *The Spirit above the Dust* (London, 1951), seems to have been the first to argue seriously that Melville had a "vision of Nothing . . . coupled simultaneously with a vision of the impersonal malevolence of the universe" (p. 133), but his reading of *Moby Dick* is in too many respects crude. The difficulty with using the idea of nonbeing to explicate Melville is that though the concept has a long philosophical history it has never been clarified into terms that make it self-evident; one can't simply mention "Nothing" and pass on to other matters. How *Melville* articulates it in his books—gives, paradoxically, form and qualities to it—is of whatever critical value the concept has.

9. Arvin, pp. 163, 165.

10. "Techniquement, *Moby Dick* a donc toutes les apparences d'une oeuvre qui essaie de rivaliser avec les forces universelles, qui cherche par sa dispersion fulgurante, sa composition en torrent, par ses obscurités et ses raccourcis à reproduire l'effet d'un monde, aux prises avec la foudre. Tel est le véritable réalisme. Il n'imite pas ce qui est mais il prétend, dans un ordre et avec des moyens littéraires, donner la même impression, accumuler au coeur des êtres la même épouvante et la même flamme qui pourraient leur venir du spectacle des créations ou des destructions cosmiques. Il y a peu d'oeuvres . . . où comme dans *Moby Dick* le langage exerce sur le lecteur une action aussi complète et aussi singulière. La phrase entraîne celui qui s'y laisse prendre sans qu'il sache où il va et où il se perd. Elle transporte des images étincelantes qui retombent avec une violence voluptueuse, n'ayant rien éclairci, laissant le paysage qu'elles ont éclairé plus sombre du feu qu'elles lui ont jeté en vain. Elle attire l'attention dans son sillage sinueux, elle l'oblige à une complète obéissance, elle lui rend familière une navigation sans espoir et sans issue, et le naufrage lui-même n'est plus qu'un accident insignifiant au prix de cette folie cruelle du langage qui dit tout et qui ne dit rien, condamné finalement au silence, après ces débauches de cris et d'images, par la simplicité de son mystère."   [Blanchot, pp. 284–86]

INDEX

Notes are sparingly indexed, the bibliography not at all. Characters in *Moby Dick* are cited only when the reference is extended, or is important to the argument developed.

WITHDRAWN